Dimensions of United States-Mexican Relations

Volume 1

Images of Mexico
in the United States

Dimensions of United States-Mexican Relations

a series

Volume 1.   *Images of Mexico in the United States*, edited by John H. Coatsworth and Carlos Rico, with contributions from Christine E. Contee, John Bailey, Carlos E. Cortés, and Gerald Greenfield.

Volume 2.   *The Economics of Interdependence: Mexico and the United States*, edited by William Glade and Cassio Luiselli, with contributions from Barry Bosworth, Francisco Gil Díaz, Rosario Green, Luis Bravo Aguilera, Guy Erb, Joseph Greenwald, Manuel Armendáriz, and B. Timothy Bennett.

Volume 3.   *Mexican Migration to the United States: Origins, Consequences, and Policy Options*, edited by Wayne Cornelius and Jorge Bustamante, with contributions from Wayne Cornelius, Manuel García y Griego, Marta Tienda, Kitty Calavita, and Jorge Bustamante.

Volume 4.   *The Drug Connection in U.S.-Mexican Relations*, edited by Marta Tienda and Guadalupe González, with contributions from Ann J. Blanken, Miguel Ruiz-Cabañas I., Richard B. Craig, and Samuel I. del Villar.

Volume 5.   *Foreign Policy in U.S.-Mexican Relations*, edited by Rosario Green and Peter H. Smith, with contributions from Guadalupe González, Lars Schoultz, Jorge Chabat, Carlos Rico, Cathryn L. Thorup, Claude Heller, and William H. Luers.

Series editors:
Rosario Green and Peter H. Smith

Images of Mexico in the United States

edited by
John H. Coatsworth and Carlos Rico

Dimensions of U.S.-Mexican Relations, Volume 1
papers prepared for the
Bilateral Commission on the Future of United States-Mexican Relations

Published by the
Center for U.S.-Mexican Studies
University of California, San Diego
1989

ISBN # 0-935391-88-6

Table of Contents

SECTION I

ATTITUDES

SECTION II

SOURCES

Dimensions of United States-Mexican Relations: Series Introduction

Rosario Green and Peter H. Smith

This volume is part of a five-volume series, *Dimensions of United States-Mexican Relations*, consisting of selected background papers originally prepared for the use of the Bilateral Commission on the Future of United States-Mexican Relations.

Appreciation of the series must begin with an understanding of its origin. The Bilateral Commission was formed in 1986 as an independent, privately funded group of prominent citizens who were seeking to make a contribution to the improvement of U.S.-Mexican relations. Early in its deliberations the Commission agreed to produce a book-length report in time for consideration by incoming presidents to be elected in 1988.

With a two-year schedule, the Commission decided to seek the opinions of expert analysts on a variety of issues—specifically, on economics (including debt, trade, and investment), migration, drugs, foreign policy, and cultural relations. In addition, of course, Commissioners read a great deal of already published material and heard testimony from numerous government officials in both Mexico and the United States.

As staff directors for the Commission, the two of us assumed responsibility for coordination of the research activity. With the assistance of an Academic Committee,[1] we organized an intensive series of workshops and solicited papers from leading experts on each of these broad topics.

Our principal purpose was to provide the Commission with a broad range of informed perspectives on key issues in U.S.-Mexican relations. We wanted to introduce its members to the terms of current debates, rather than buttress conventional wisdoms; we sought to acquaint them with the broadest possible range of policy alternatives, rather than bias the discussion in favor of any particular view.

As a result, many Commissioners do not agree with the opinions expressed in these papers—just as some of the authors may disagree with parts of the Commission's report, published in English as *The Challenge of Interdependence: Mexico and the United States* (University Press of America, 1988).[2]

Accordingly, the publication of this series does not necessarily represent the viewpoints of the Commission or its members, and the papers herein do not simply provide supporting documentation for positions and recommendations of the Commission. The *Dimensions of United States-Mexican Relations* series represents an outgrowth of the same initiative that resulted in the Commission's report, but in other senses it is separate from it.

As we developed our research program on behalf of the Bilateral Commission, we nonetheless sought to make useful contributions to scholarly discourse on U.S.-Mexican relations. In this regard we had three goals:

One was to encourage the application of *comparative perspectives* to the study of U.S.-Mexican relations. Much of the work in this field has tended to concentrate on properties of the bilateral relationship alone and to assume, and often to assert, that the U.S.-Mexican connection has been "unique." It goes without saying, however, that you cannot determine the uniqueness of a relationship without comparing it to others. This we invited our authors to do.

Second was to encourage appropriate *attention to the United States*. We believe that much of the literature tends to concentrate

---

[1]The members were: Jorge Bustamante, John Coatsworth, Wayne Cornelius, William Glade, Guadalupe González, Cassio Luiselli, Carlos Rico, and Marta Tienda.
[2]The Spanish-language version appeared under the title *El desafío de la interdependencia: México y Estados Unidos* (Mexico: Fondo de Cultura Económica, 1988).

too much on Mexico, on Mexico's problems, and on Mexican contributions to the state of the relationship. We wanted to correct that imbalance and, at the same time, to promote the study of the United States by Mexican students and scholars.[3]

Third was to encourage analysts to spell out the *policy implications* of their work. Academic investigation and primary research have enormous value, of course, but we hoped to provide an opportunity for scholars to speak as directly as possible to the policy-making community. Accordingly, we asked each contributor to provide practical policy recommendations; in addition, we obtained some papers from specialists with policy experience and authority.

With such criteria in mind we solicited and obtained forty-eight papers that were presented at about a dozen workshops in 1987 and early 1988.[4] These presentations proved to be of great use to the Bilateral Commission. With the aid of the Academic Committee, we then defined a set of topics for the volumes in this series. We selected papers for inclusion in the series primarily on the basis of their relationship to these particular subjects. This led us, regrettably, to exclude many fine papers from this collection. But our purpose has been to produce anthologies with thematic coherence as well as substantive originality, and we hope to have achieved that goal.

We conclude with an expression of thanks to all of our authors, especially to those whose papers are not in these volumes; to members of the Commission and its co-chairmen, Hugo Margáin and William D. Rogers; to our colleagues on the Academic Committee; to officers at the Ford Foundation who made possible this enterprise. Sandra del Castillo, Lee Dewey, Will Heller, Blanca Salgado, Gerardo Santos, and Arturo Sarukhan all made invaluable contributions to the editing and production of these volumes; to them our heartfelt gratitude.

Mexico City

La Jolla

---

[3]Indeed, one of the most alarming findings of the Commission relates to the decline of U.S. studies in Mexico. See *Challenge*, ch. 6.

[4]A complete listing of all papers appears in Appendix II of the Commission's report, *The Challenge of Interdependence*. Papers not included in this series may be published elsewhere and are available upon request; please send written inquiries to the U.S. Office of the Bilateral Commission, Institute of the Americas, 10111 North Torrey Pines Road, La Jolla, CA 92037.

1

Images of Mexico in the United States: Introduction

John H. Coatsworth and Carlos M. Rico Ferrat

What difference do images make? Hallowed traditions of contemporary scholarship interpret international relations as the pursuit and result of raw power. Economic might and military prowess share and determine the balance (or imbalance) of power. Ideological systems and cultural perceptions offer subsequent justifications, turning de facto dominance into superstructural "hegemony," but they do not have genuinely independent influence. Images and stereotypes are essentially secondary matters, according to this outlook, continuing grist for the mill of well-intentioned educators who so earnestly lament impediments to cross-cultural "understanding"—but not serious material for hard-nosed analysts of international realities. Decisions, not images, make the world go 'round.

But images affect decisions. For this simple reason the study of perceptions—images, stereotypes, reputations, prestige, credibility, and the like—in international affairs rightly lays claim to a tradition as venerable and distinguished as the analysis of the decision-making process itself. Perceptions (correct or incorrect) of the nature, capacities, and intentions of friends as well as adversaries are important in almost every international exchange or transaction. The behavior of international actors is conditioned by the cultural filters through which each receives and interprets information about the other players. Culturally conditioned images, even (or especially!) stereotypes, thus exert a powerful effect upon decision-making.

The shared language and imagery of the political elite, the detailed knowledge of the experts on which they rely, and the more diffuse impressions that dominate at the broadest level of society do not have the same practical implications. At times when a particular bilateral relationship is proceeding "normally," and thus attracting little high-level or public attention, policy formation and management devolve to a handful of bureaucrats who usually have more (though not necessarily adequate) knowledge of the foreign country in question. Also involved are those nongovernmental actors whose interests are immediately and directly affected by the management of the relationship.

This situation can change radically—when the degree of priority assigned to the bilateral relation on the agenda of public policy is increased, or when a greater number of nongovernmental participants develop a significant interest in the relationship. When a crisis develops, on the one hand, higher authorities with less direct experience of the country in question may become actively involved in policy-making and management. The familiarity and knowledge developed by bureaucratic specialization thus become only one of the elements entering into the process through which these higher authorities formulate policies. If the key decision-makers have relatively accurate perceptions of their foreign counterpart, then their lack of specific detail or concrete information creates only minor problems which are relatively easy to solve. If, however, neither their education nor their practical experience have given them much understanding of the "other," then their decisions may be considerably influenced by the images and stereotypes which they have taken from the cultural storehouse of their society.

When the number of nongovernmental participants in a bilateral relationship grows significantly, on the other hand, three further types of situations can emerge in which such images play an important role in the policy process:

- First, state action may be in greater or lesser degree constrained by the images dominant in society at large, especially when controversial policies or critical conjunctures force public authorities to resort to "diplomacy directed at their own population" in the management of a bilateral relationship. Such strategies reflect the existence of reciprocal channels of influence between policymakers and interest groups or the public at large. The opinions of nongovernmental participants limit the space for maneuvering by the government.

- Second, nongovernmental actors can participate directly, on their own terms and in their own ways, in shaping the bilateral relationship itself. In this context, the role of "images of the other" is relevant not only as it constitutes one of the factors that condition public policy, but also as a central source of the transnational activity that shapes and defines the conditions to which policymakers must respond.

- Third, competing interest groups vitally involved in diverse aspects of a bilateral relationship can exert influence over, or even "capture," portions of the governmental apparatus where routine decisions are made. Unstable coalitions of interest and political fortune then arise to vie for the attention of higher authorities. In this intermediate kind of situation, the mobilization of public support on behalf of sectional or particularistic causes (in the context of bureaucratic indiscipline) can then lead to the invocation of cultural stereotypes and biased imagery as competing groups pressure for favorable political outcomes.

Thus, the study (and manipulation) of cultural imagery, particularly in situations of heightened public priority and private attention, has political implications that go far beyond the simple analysis of stereotypes which—in and of themselves, no matter how misleading or insulting—have a limited impact on the management of foreign relations. Nevertheless, the scant attention paid to this subject during periods of "normality" in a bilateral relationship sharply limits knowledge about these phenomena and their potentially destabilizing impact on the conduct of foreign relations.

As though in confirmation of this pattern, we have produced this book under conditions of increased priority and attention to U.S.-Mexican relations, direct implications for the behavior of the state and private players, and scarce scientific knowledge about the roles of cultural images.

ATTENTION TO MEXICO IN THE UNITED STATES

The last few years have shown a marked increase in the interest and attention devoted to Mexico by diverse sectors of U.S. society. The chapter by John Bailey in this volume traces with precision and clarity the development of this phenomenon in the press and the electronic news media. But the scope of this increasing attention to Mexico goes well beyond the media. A number of

the principal "think tanks" and a large portion of the educated
public in the United States have begun to devote more time and
resources to following Mexico's internal developments and foreign
policies in recent years, due to the widespread and growing con-
viction that Mexico is important to U.S. domestic and international
interests.

The amount of attention devoted to Mexico in the major U.S.
foreign policy journals and forums is much greater than five or ten
years ago. In the course of the U.S. presidential campaign of 1988,
Mexico (along with the Central American crisis) was virtually the
only Latin American country to receive any degree of attention.
This attention was particularly evident in the documents produced
by committees, think tanks, lobbying organizations, and other
private organizations seeking to influence the behavior of the new
U.S. administration. Many of the high-level efforts to develop
"bipartisan" views on U.S. foreign policy issues put Mexico in a
place of top priority. For example, an article published jointly by
Henry Kissinger and Cyrus Vance argued that:

> Mexico may well present the most challenging
> problem for the United States in the western hemi-
> sphere. Most Americans appreciate the importance
> of Mexico to the United States. However, it is very
> difficult to know how to deal with the complex
> relationship.... It would be unrealistic to assume
> that there is a simple, global solution for all of the
> issues in such a complex problem. We believe, how-
> ever, that Mexican-American relations deserve high
> priority.[1]

In another effort, also undertaken by important figures on the
U.S. political scene, both Democratic as well as Republican, the
same idea was repeated:

> U.S. relations with Mexico continue to be among
> the most difficult and important of all the foreign
> policy problems that will confront the next
> President.
>
> Mexico is our third largest trading partner, our
> largest source of energy imports, and our largest

---

[1]"Bipartisan Objectives for Foreign Policy," *Foreign Affairs* 66,5 (Summer, 1988),
917-18.

unprotected border. The system of government in Mexico carried the country from its revolution until about a decade ago, but this system has not been able to adapt to cultural, social, economic and political changes in Mexico itself.

Mexico has grave economic problems. It has a massive debt that cannot be met. It cannot produce the jobs necessary to meet its population increase. It is a country increasingly divided economically, with the more northern one-third of the country more and more identified with and connected to the United States and the other two-thirds are becoming more and more depressed economically and less and less stable politically.

We believe that if the United States should have to face the reality of pervasive instability on our southern border, the impact would be massive—unprecedented in our modern history. A threat so close to the U.S. would consume attention and affect the way the U.S. looks at the rest of the world.

In addition, we believe that Mexico deserves to be considered as more than simply one of the countries in the State Department's Latin American bureau; it deserves a special place under someone of substantial stature.[2]

Efforts directed more specifically to the analysis of U.S. policy towards Latin America argued uniformly in the same direction. Mexico was in all cases described as an area of high priority, if not the highest priority for the United States. It is noteworthy that these types of recommendations encompassed practically the whole spectrum of the U.S. policy community. The same idea was repeated in many academic works by U.S. scholars interested in influencing policy. For example, former Carter administration official Robert Pastor has argued that: "Today, excepting the Soviet Union for strategic reasons and Japan for economic ones, Mexico probably has a greater capacity to affect the United States than any other country."[3] Meanwhile, analysts mainly concerned with U.S. national

---

[2]*Presidential Agenda 1988.*
[3]Robert A. Pastor and Jorge G. Castañeda, *Limits to Friendship: The United States and Mexico* (New York: Alfred A. Knopf, 1988), p. 5.

security have repeated the same message: the United States should pay more attention to Mexico.

But it is not only the press and specialists that refer with greater and greater frequency to Mexico. U.S. public opinion is increasingly consulted with respect to its neighbor to the south. The image that emerges from public opinion polls, such as those described by Bailey and Christine Contee in their chapters for this volume, is complex and to some extent contradictory. What should be underlined, in any case, is the cumulative effect of these overall changes: the Mexican-United States bilateral relationship has attracted such high-level attention and engages so many non-governmental actors that an understanding of prevailing images and perceptions on the U.S. side has acquired great importance.

It is for this reason that we should not only be interested in the image the U.S. government has of Mexico but also that of the so-called "educated public" closest to power. It has become crucial to understand how the U.S. public "sees" Mexico. Description and interpretation of images and stereotypes should be accompanied by analysis of their sources. The education, both formal and informal, of U.S. citizens about the realities that rule the rest of the world has been justly questioned by many U.S. observers.[4] Mexico is not the only country that is interpreted through profoundly distorted lenses. With the exception of countries much more familiar to the U.S. public, like those of western Europe, or to some extent Canada, U.S. perceptions of the rest of the world leave much to be desired.

Yet this is not the first time that the U.S. media has developed a taste for covering events in Mexico. As Carlos Cortés's chapter demonstrates in the case of U.S. cinema, events such as the Mexican Revolution had a notable impact on U.S. perceptions of Mexico. The same is true of the print media. At the time of Mexico's expropriation of its foreign-owned petroleum industry in 1938, one of the affected companies—the Standard Oil Company—commissioned a survey of editorial opinion subsequently published under the suggestive title "Mexico at the Bar of Public Opinion." Since that era Mexican issues have received extensive coverage in leading U.S. daily newspapers on a sporadic but recurrent basis.

---

[4]See papers by Christine Contee and Gerald Greenfield, in this volume; and the report of the Bilateral Commission on the Future of United States-Mexican Relations, *The Challenge of Interdependence: Mexico and the United States* (Lanham, MD: University Press of America, 1988), ch. 6.

Although recent coverage has not been directly sponsored by interest groups affected by what happens in Mexico or by the policies of the Mexican government, U.S. reporting has undoubtedly been marked by a critical tone, in which sometimes inadequate perceptions have been mixed with more judicious and balanced evaluations of Mexican realities. This can be seen both in the commentaries of the mass media as well as in the work of diverse "think tanks," and even in a good many works of U.S. academics.

Does the new prominence of Mexico in U.S. public affairs stem mainly from conjunctural or transitory developments that may disappear or at least diminish over the medium term? Or, on the contrary, does Mexico's greater prominence in the United States come from more or less permanent and irreversible trends in the bilateral relationship itself?

SOURCES OF INCREASED U.S. ATTENTION TO MEXICO

A number of factors help explain the growing U.S. interest in Mexico. The ever more intense interaction between the economies and societies of both countries is perhaps the strongest and deepest of these new developments. Every day the number of U.S. citizens who, in one way or another, have direct contact with Mexico grows. But there are other factors of great importance. Among them is the important role that Mexico now plays not only in U.S. foreign policy, but even in U.S. domestic affairs.

It is not surprising that one of the first waves of increased attention in the immediate past was linked to Mexico's emergence in the late 1970s as a prominent player on the international energy scene, exactly at the same time that the U.S. government defined the energy problem as an area of top national priority. At other times, it has been not opportunity but fear that has led the United States to rediscover its neighbor to the south. The issue of drug trafficking is frequently mentioned in this context and has certainly taken a place of high priority in U.S. perceptions of Mexico, especially since 1985. In the case of drugs there developed a double image of Mexico: it was both the *source* of a high-priority problem for the United States and, on the other hand, a potential *solution* as well.

The foreign debt crisis and the austerity policies carried out by the Mexican government in response to it deserve special

attention because of the deep impact they have had on the imagination of key private and governmental actors in the United States.
Three distinct dimensions of this impact can be mentioned. First,
the size of the Mexican foreign debt made U.S. observers aware,
for the first time, of the effect that Mexico could have on the
standard and quality of living in the United States. In 1982, it
became evident in a dramatic way that Mexico's inability to pay
its debt could have a profound impact on the U.S. and international
financial system. The shape of the debt problem has changed
significantly in recent years, but that new awareness of U.S.
vulnerability has already had an effect on U.S.-Mexican relations.

A second way in which the problem of the debt served to
awaken growing U.S. interest in Mexico was through concern over
the potential effect of the Mexican financial crisis and the meas-
ures adopted to confront it on what traditionally has been considered as the most basic of all U.S. interests in Mexico: stability. Ever
since World War II, the stability of Mexico's political and economic
system has proven to be fundamentally compatible with U.S. interests. During the 1980s many observers in the United States
concluded that Mexico's stability would be impossible to sustain
in view of pressures generated by the debt crisis and the economic
difficulties that followed. These worries were nourished by the U.S.
preoccupation with another geographic sphere intimately associ-
ated with U.S. perceptions of Mexico: Central America. And this
brings us to the third set of factors that helped heighten the U.S.
interest in Mexico: developments taking place in the rest of Latin
America.

Of all the changes occurring in Latin America over the past
decade—tumultuous transitions toward democracy, economic and
financial crises, social decay amid renewed cultural effervescence—
the Central American problem has been undoubtedly the most
important to U.S. policymakers and the U.S. public. While Mexico's
independent foreign policy in Central America projected an image
not easily squared with that of a country in crisis and on the verge
of collapse, the U.S. government expressed increasing concern with
Mexican conditions. With the objective of justifying policies that
did not seem to correspond to a pragmatic definition of U.S. interests, many in the United States defended the policies of the Reagan
administration in Central America by invoking the Mexican variable. The main idea was that U.S. policy toward the isthmus was
not in the final analysis motivated by the scarcely credible threat
to U.S. security posed by these tiny countries, but rather by the

need to guarantee the security of the most important "domino" in the region: Mexico. For various conservative sectors it was particularly irritating that the country that justified their concern did not share their diagnosis. Mexican foreign policy in Central America thus contributed to raising the attention Mexico received in those circles.

Developments in South America during the second half of the 1980s also had an impact on U.S. perceptions of Mexico. Political openings in key countries such as Brazil and Argentina not only captured U.S. attention, but also tended to refocus the U.S. imagination on the idea of democracy. As part of its efforts to sway a reluctant U.S. public, the Reagan administration raised the banner of democracy in the Central American case. The democratic transition in most of the principal South American countries, along with the Philippines, reinforced this idea. Mexico could hardly remain outside this trend. Only a few years earlier, the Mexican political system had seemed clearly more open than those in South America; but the formation of liberal multi-party democracies in most of these countries during the 1980s caused Mexico's image to fall in comparison. This was particularly important because of internal developments taking place south of the Rio Grande. This brings us to the last set of factors that help to explain the growing U.S. attention towards Mexico.

The evolution of Mexico's political affairs, not just its economic traumas, has contributed an abundance of news stories to transmit and new phenomena to interpret. From the emergence of the Partido de Acción Nacional (PAN) as a powerful and effective opposition in the north of the country to the exciting 1988 electoral campaign of the Frente Democrático Nacional's presidential candidate, Cuauhtémoc Cárdenas, the Mexican political scene has recently shown an unprecedented dynamism, clearly moving it in the same democratic direction as the rest of Latin America.[5]

Increasing interactions between the two economies and societies; growth in the importance of Mexican issues on both the U.S. foreign and domestic U.S. policy agendas; a situation, both economic and political, not only complex and interesting but also potentially threatening to U.S. interests; a changing regional context

---

[5]For discussion of these trends see Wayne A. Cornelius, Judith Gentleman, and Peter H. Smith (eds.), *Mexico's Alternative Political Futures* (La Jolla: Center for U.S.-Mexican Studies, University of California at San Diego, 1989).

clearly related to Mexico's political dynamism—these are some of
the reasons that help explain the significant change in the amount
of attention paid to Mexico in the United States. None of these
factors are likely to disappear in the near or even medium term
future.

MEXICAN PERCEPTIONS OF THE UNITED STATES

The increase in U.S. awareness and interest in Mexico have not
substantially changed the asymmetry that characterizes the
Mexican-U.S. relationship. The United States is much more a real
and concrete part of Mexican reality and political discourse than
vice versa. In fact, the United States constitutes a crucial variable
in the very definition of Mexico's modern political culture.

The proximity of a country not only much more powerful, but
also prepared to use its disproportionate power for its own ends,
has clearly marked the process of formation of a Mexican national
identity. That sensation of constant threat has been much less
present for the U.S. When the United States has felt threatened,
Mexico has not been the cause. It is not only that Mexicans look
more to the past than their neighbors, but also that the United States
holds a central place in the history of Mexico; Mexico's place in
U.S. history is quite limited.

The presence of the United States in the print and electronic
media of Mexico is also in no way comparable to that of Mexico in
the U.S. media. Not a day passes in Mexico without reference by
the major media to developments north of the Rio Grande. Despite
all of the recent growth in attention to Mexico in the United States,
no comparable interest in Mexican affairs exists in the U.S. media.

A final element of this asymmetry should be emphasized. The
United States constitutes an almost unavoidable presence in the
daily lives of most Mexicans. The music that is heard in the main
urban centers of the country, the companies that dominate the
billboards and television advertising, the entertainment and news
broadcasts of the major media—all of these refer almost by neces-
sity to the United States, creating a sense, however partial and
distorted, of familiarity with U.S. society and culture.

The absence of studies analyzing Mexican perceptions of the
United States is thus all the more striking than it would be if the
United States were not such an inescapable part of Mexico's

political culture and daily life. In part, this lack of information and analysis offers yet another reflection of the asymmetry in power and resources. With barely one-eighth the per capita income of the United States, Mexico has been able to train fewer scholars and experts on all subjects, even in such important fields as survey research and the analysis of public opinion. This lack of analysis of Mexican perceptions of the United States is also due to the greater importance of proprietary information in Mexico. Government agencies and foreign embassies regularly conduct public opinion surveys, but their results often remain private.[6]

Some interesting work has been published on the image of the United States in Mexican educational materials. The study by Josefina Vázquez of U.S.-related materials in commercially-produced primary and secondary school textbooks is a notable example.[7] Less edifying has been a long debate over the treatment of the United States in the free textbooks distributed to primary schools by Mexico's public education ministry. Despite their exceptionally balanced treatment of such controversial issues as the U.S.-Mexican war (1846-48) and the subsequent treatment of Mexican citizens in the territories seized by the United States, some U.S. analysts continue to complain that the free textbooks slight the United States by failing to acknowledge or identify as U.S. contributions many notable U.S. achievements in science and technology.[8]

Analysis of the image of the United States in the print and electronic media is lacking in Mexico because the U.S. image is largely a U.S. product. Except for occasional commentary, nearly all of the news printed or broadcast in Mexico about the United States is provided by U.S. media. The same is true in the entertainment media. Images of the United States in film and on television come largely from U.S. sources. What are lacking, of course, are studies of the impressions and opinions created among Mexicans by these U.S. sources.

---

[6]For the exception that proves the rule see the essay by Barbara Farah (of the *New York Times*) reporting on a U.S. poll about Mexican views of the United States, paper presented to the workshop on cultural relations of the Bilateral Commission (October 1987).

[7]Josefina Vázquez, "The Image of the United States in Mexican Textbooks," paper presented to the workshop on cultural relations of the Bilateral Commission (October 1987).

[8]Vesta Manning, "Images of the United States in Mexico's *Libros de Texto Gratuitos*," paper presented to the workshop on cultural relations of the Bilateral Commission (October 1987).

Mexicans have frequently found it difficult to deal with the image of themselves reflected by the U.S. mirror. For example, one of the books that helped most to shape the prevailing image of Mexico among the educated public of the United States[9] was sharply criticized south of the Rio Grande at the very time when, in the United States, the same work was thought to be a major contribution to the understanding of Mexico. U.S. press coverage has also received critical reviews in Mexico, though it should be pointed out that critics of the press have also been found north of the border in recent years.

IN THIS VOLUME

The essays in this book come from a workshop on "cultural relations" sponsored by the Bilateral Commission on the Future of United States-Mexican Relations and held at the University of Chicago in October 1987. Presentations on that occasion included outstanding papers by Barbara Farah and Josefina Vázquez on Mexican perceptions of the United States, as well as in-depth analyses of the human and financial resources dedicated to U.S. studies in Mexico and to Mexican studies in the United States. To sharpen the focus of this volume, however, we here include only those papers devoted to the study of images of Mexico in the United States.

The opening chapters, by John Bailey and Christine Contee, provide a clear picture of the *state* of U.S. public opinion. They also suggest that the U.S. media have not dispelled and in some respects may even have reinforced negative impressions of Mexico among the U.S. public. As Bailey points out, however, there is no evidence to support the notion, still widely held by many educated Mexican citizens, that the U.S. government (or a collection of U.S. private interests) has been involved in orchestrating negative reporting on Mexico in the U.S. news media. "Pack journalism"—the pressure to go after a story once it has received prominent attention elsewhere in the media—explains much of what Mexicans are sometimes inclined to view as much more sinister.

---

[9]Alan Riding, *Distant Neighbors: A Portrait of the Mexicans* (New York: Alfred A. Knopf, 1985).

Our other two essays analyze *sources* of popular opinion. Gerald Greenfield explores the treatment of Mexico in U.S. textbooks and teaching materials. And Carlos Cortés traces the slow (though, he would argue, clearly perceptible) progress made by the U.S. film industry in emancipating itself from the degrading stereotypes that characterized many Hollywood productions some decades ago.

Grounds for hope exist nonetheless. Polling results, such as those analyzed by Contee, suggest that "familiarity breeds respect." U.S. citizens who have visited Mexico, even briefly as tourists, tend to view Mexico in a more positive light than those who have never traveled there. This makes it all the more regrettable that Mexico's economic crisis, together with funding problems north of the border, have combined to reduce the number of student, academic, and other scholarly exchanges between the two countries in recent years.[10] In the long run, improvement in the bilateral relationship at the level of public policy as well as private interaction will depend in large part on how thoroughly the citizens of the two countries are able to exploit their proximity to dispel unjustified fears and to build new images that credit their neighbors' positive qualities.

---

[10]See John H. Coatsworth, "Student, Academic, and Cultural Exchanges between Mexico and the United States," paper presented to workshop on cultural relations of the Bilateral Commission (October 1987).

SECTION

I

ATTITUDES

2

U.S. Perceptions of
United States-Mexican Relations

Christine E. Contee

In 1986, the Overseas Development Council, in collaboration with InterAction, a consortium of U.S. private voluntary agencies, undertook a comprehensive study of U.S. public opinion and attitudes with regard to developing countries and U.S. relations with them. The study touched upon a broad range of topics, including the causes of poverty and underdevelopment in the Third World, prospects for development, regional problems, U.S. interests in the Third World and in development, and U.S. aid, security, trade, investment, and financial policies toward the Third World. The project's two primary objectives were to gather data on an area of public opinion that had been relatively neglected for many years and examine factors that may motivate or inhibit public support of U.S. efforts to assist Third World development.

This study was not specifically designed to probe the attitudes of the U.S. public toward Mexico or on the relationship between that country and the United States, so this paper is based on a small number of the questions asked. The Overseas Development Council has a long-standing interest in U.S.-Mexican relations. Since 1979, the Council's U.S.-Mexico Project has worked to improve both communication and policy in U.S.-Mexican relations, serving as a center for policy analysis on critical issues in the binational relationship and as the major forum for discussion in Washington, D.C. for policymakers from the public and private sectors of both countries. Therefore, a number of questions included in the study focused on the relationship between the United States and Mexico. Moreover, several of the questions asked in general terms on subjects such as foreign policy priorities, development problems, U.S. trade policy, and the debt crisis are directly relevant to U.S. views on key issues in U.S.-Mexican relations.

The ODC/InterAction collaborative project included four distinct research components designed and implemented by the Strategic Information Research Corporation in consultation with the co-sponsors.[1] First, telephone interviews were conducted with a random sample of 2,400 Americans on a range of issues pertaining to development and U.S. relations with the Third World. In this text, these respondents are referred to as the "general public."

The second phase of the project consisted of telephone interviews with five hundred individuals in the United States who are or have been active in political or social issues (referred to as "activists" throughout this report). They were questioned about U.S.-Third World issues and the motivating factors for becoming actively involved in supporting U.S. development cooperation efforts. These individuals are not necessarily opinion leaders, but they are people who make things happen in communities around the country through business, religious, political, and community action groups as well as school and college boards, church councils, and political campaigns. The activists in this study are not necessarily involved in Third World issues or international affairs generally, but they represent types of citizens who are more likely to become involved in such efforts.

The third and fourth stages of the project involved interviews with thirteen members of Congress and congressional staff and four focus group discussions held around the country. These are not referred to in this paper because the issue of Mexico or U.S.-Mexican relations was not a focus of discussion.

---

[1]For fuller explanation of the methodology of each research component, see appendix.

OVERVIEW: PERCEPTIONS OF U.S.-THIRD WORLD RELATIONS
AND DEVELOPING COUNTRIES

Before addressing U.S. views specific to Mexico and the bilateral relationship, it is useful to briefly examine attitudes toward U.S. relations with the Third World as a whole. One can only conjecture that opinions with regard to general topics will hold in specific instances, but at least two factors indicate that one can learn about U.S. views on U.S.-Mexican issues by looking at the public's perceptions of U.S.-Third World relations in general. First, survey responses were consistent on several key issues both when broached in general terms and when specifically referred to in terms of U.S.-Mexican relations. For example, most respondents did not favor vigorous U.S. government action to resolve Third World debt, nor did they perceive debt to be the most important, or even the second most critical, issue in U.S.-Mexican relations.

Second, most of the public is poorly informed about foreign policy as well as about developing countries. A large segment of the population is probably equally unfamiliar with the political and economic specifics of the U.S.-Mexican relationship. Therefore, their perceptions of Mexico do not differ radically from their perceptions of developing countries in general or of U.S.-Third World issues broadly defined. An important caveat here is that more Americans have traveled to Mexico than to any other developing nation, implying at least a certain degree of familiarity with the country and its people that is lacking vis-à-vis any other Third World nation. Despite this factor, and in the absence of a larger study focusing in greater depth on U.S. views toward Mexico, it is probably useful to consider general views toward Mexico in the light of perceptions toward the Third World as a whole.

Priority of Domestic Issues

The U.S. public places a far higher priority on domestic well-being than on foreign policy problems. For most Americans, international issues generally rank fairly low compared to other concerns. For example, in the ODC/InterAction study 64 percent of the general public surveyed independently identified domestic "bread and butter" issues—unemployment, the national budget deficit, or the general state of the U.S. economy—as the most pressing.[2] When asked to rate the importance of a number of specific issues confronting the government, respondents assigned the lowest priority to reducing poverty and hunger in other countries and to lowering the trade deficit, while giving high priority to public education, checking crime, and alleviating domestic poverty (table 1).

Table 1. Priority of U.S. National Problems

"Using our scale where 1 means lowest priority and 10 means top priority, please tell me how you would rate these issues the government has to deal with." Asked of the general population; results given in percentages.

	Very Important (8-10)	Somewhat Important (4-7)	Not Important (1-3)
Public education	61	31	6
Dealing with crime	59	33	6
Helping the poor in the United States	56	33	10
Reducing the national budget deficit	53	35	10
International arms control	52	34	11
Unemployment	50	39	9
Reducing the trade deficit	34	51	9
Reducing poverty and hunger in other countries	19	52	27

Foreign Policy Priorities

When Americans do focus on foreign relations, they are generally much more concerned about U.S. relations with traditional allies or adversaries than about Third World countries. Asked to rank several countries according to their importance to the United States, approximately two-thirds of the general public rated Great Britain and the USSR as very important. Less than half gave this rating to China and Mexico, and less than one-fifth to Nigeria and India (table 2). The responses to this question are discussed in detail below.

---

[2]In response to this open ended question, the largest proportion of respondents (35 percent) cited international terrorism as one of the biggest problems facing the United States. Although the 14 April 1986 U.S. attack on Libya occurred while the general population survey was being conducted, there was little difference between the responses recorded before and after the event. Even before the attack on Libya, however, the media were focusing a great deal of attention on international terrorism, no doubt with some impact on responses.

Table 2. Importance of Selected Countries to the United States

"Using our scale where 1 means not at all important and 10 means very important, please tell me how important you feel each of these countries is to the United States." Asked of the general population; results given in percentages.

	Very Important (8-10)	Somewhat Important (4-7)	Not Important (1-3)	Don't Know/ No Answer
Great Britain	61	29	8	2
Soviet Union	60	21	17	2
China	48	40	10	2
Mexico	40	45	13	2
Nigeria	14	49	30	7
India	13	53	30	4

U.S. Interests in the Third World

Although other national and international priorities conflict with or limit the concern of activists and the general public about U.S.-Third World or development issues, a majority do perceive the United States to have humanitarian, economic, and political/ strategic interests in developing countries.

Humanitarian concerns. Most Americans believe that the United States has a humanitarian responsibility to help developing countries and their people. For example, 89 percent of those surveyed in the general population agreed with the statement: "Wherever people are hungry or poor, we ought to do what we can to help them;" 73 percent of the activists agreed that: "Because we live in one of the richest countries in the world, Americans have a responsibility to help improve conditions in poorer countries."

The overall survey results indicated that the most important reason both the general public and activists support public and private efforts to assist Third World countries in their development efforts is humanitarianism. Among certain demographic subgroups, concern about U.S.-Third World economic, social, or political relations accompanies feelings of compassion or responsibility. But for the majority of Americans, humanitarian concern appears to be the major basis for interest in helping the Third World. Other mutual interests are not widely perceived or understood.

Political Interests. Americans tend to view the Third World as a dangerous arena of conflict between the Soviet Union and the

United States. Over one-half (59 percent) of those surveyed in the general population agreed strongly with the statement that "Soviet aggression in the Third World is a serious problem for the United States," while 26 percent agreed somewhat. Republicans, older Americans, and those living in the southern United States[3] tended to strongly agree with the statement more often than others.

Asked to rate some possible long-term problems of Third World countries, nearly one-half (48 percent) of the activists rated the threat of communism as very serious, and an additional 37 percent rated it as a somewhat serious problem. Again, those who rated the threat of communism as very serious tended to live in lower-income households, to be older, to live in the South, and to have received less formal education.

Probing specifically on the issue of communism in Mexico, a survey conducted by Market Opinion Research in April 1988 found that 61 percent of the public believed that the presence of a pro-Soviet, communist government in Mexico would pose a very serious threat to the national security of the United States.[4] However, it was evident in the same survey that the public does not believe such a threat currently exists. Only 5 percent of the public identified the Mexican government as a pro-Soviet communist government; 48 percent identified it as democratic, 25 percent as neither communist nor democratic, and 22 percent had no opinion. Finally, when asked whether the Soviet Union is or is not supporting a communist revolution against the government of Mexico, only 14 percent responded positively, 53 percent said such a revolution was not being supported by the USSR, and 33 percent had no opinion.

Most of the general public surveyed in the ODC/InterAction study believed that it is in the U.S. interest to foster political reforms within developing countries in areas such as human rights reforms and free elections. U.S. activists displayed a significant degree of cynicism regarding the objectives of industrial-country policies toward the Third World with 51 percent saying that "governments of wealthier nations get involved in Third World countries mostly to take advantage of them."

Economic Interests. At a general level, most of those surveyed appeared to be aware of economic linkages between the United

---

[3]Regions correspond to the U.S. Census Bureau regions.
[4]Survey conducted by Market Opinion Research for Americans Talk Security, 25 April-1 May 1988; data from the Roper Center for Public Opinion Research.

States and the Third World. When asked whether the economies of countries in the Third World affect the U.S. economy, one-quarter (26 percent) of the general public responded that Third World economies affect the U.S. economy a great deal and nearly half (48 percent) said the U.S. economy was affected somewhat.

A majority of the U.S. public also perceived this interrelationship to hold potential benefits for both the developing countries and the United States. Thus, 75 percent of the general public agreed with the statement: "If the United States helps the Third World, we will benefit in the long run." Two-thirds (65 percent) rejected the statement that: "It is against U.S. interests to help countries in the Third World because they will compete with us economically and politically." More men than women—and more upper-income than lower-income respondents—perceived such long-term benefits and rejected the idea that concern about future competition should curtail U.S. efforts. By a narrower margin (55-43 percent), a majority of the activists agreed that: "Helping Third World countries is in our self-interest because as they develop, they will buy American products."

When questioned about specific U.S. trade or finance policies, however, most respondents were not supportive of policies that might promote such mutual well-being. Eighty percent of the activists surveyed agreed that the United States should take care of its own financial problems before actively helping to reduce the foreign debt of Third World countries; and 60 percent of the general public said the United States should restrict imports from the developing countries until the U.S. trade deficit is lowered. From these responses, it seems that although the U.S. public may be aware of the concept that global linkages are beneficial over the long term, they tend to perceive current international economic relations as a "negative sum game," in which jobs and markets are lost for the United States. Moreover, neither the general public nor the activists appear to see much of a linkage between domestic and international economic problems or policies; for example, the relationship between the U.S. financial situation and developing countries' debt problems does not seem to be widely understood.

Further evidence of a weak understanding of economic linkages is provided in the reasons both the general public and the activists offered for supporting U.S. economic assistance to developing countries. Among those who supported such programs, 53 percent of the general public and 64 percent of the activists volunteered reasons such as humanitarian concern or a feeling of responsibility. Such economic reasons for supporting aid as fostering economic stability and growth in the Third World, bringing economic benefits to the United States and the developing countries, and promoting self-sufficiency in the Third World were cited by only 14 percent of the general public and 20 percent of the activists.[5]

Perceptions of Third World Problems

Americans are very aware of disease, hunger, and poverty experienced by people in Third World countries, and most do not believe that the situation is improving. Only 32 percent of the general public in the survey believed that living conditions in the poor countries of the world are better today than they were ten years ago. More than half (56 percent) of the respondents expressed the view that Third World living conditions have stagnated or deteriorated over the past decade.[6]

Most of those surveyed perceived poverty in developing countries to be caused by factors beyond the control of the people in those countries. Asked to rate the severity of some long-term problems that Third World countries may face, the activists considered the proposition that people do not work hard enough to be the least important problem of those enumerated; only one-fifth considered this to be a very serious problem. Nearly three-quarters rated disease, hunger, and poor health care as extremely serious. A majority also perceived overpopulation, corrupt governments, and illiteracy to be serious problems. Other problems considered more critical than "people who don't work hard enough" were the threat of communism, lack of adequate resources such as water and fertile land, and the absence of democracy.

Members of the general public were asked to describe in their own words the major problems facing the developing regions of Africa, Asia, and Latin America. In relation to Africa,

---

[5]Political and strategic rationales for supporting U.S. economic assistance, such as making and keeping allies, discouraging communism, fostering democracy, and promoting world peace, were volunteered by 28 percent of the public and 21 percent of the activists.

[6]Thirty-five percent said that conditions have remained about the same and 21 percent said they have declined.

nearly one-half (48 percent) of the public named hunger and poverty as the major problems. Other critical problems named included racial discrimination (cited by 17 percent), lack of technical know-how (13 percent), bad leadership (13 percent,) and overpopulation (8 percent). Asked to focus on Asia, the general public again cited hunger and poverty as the most crucial problems (24 percent), followed by overpopulation (17 percent), poor or unstable governance (10 percent), and lack of know-how (7 percent).

When considering Latin America, the public cited hunger and poverty most frequently (21 percent) although these problems were less often cited in relation to Latin America than in the cases of Africa and Asia. Internal political problems were also mentioned often: bad leadership and exploitation of those in power were cited by 11 percent of the respondents; unstable governments by 7 percent; and civil war and communist subversion by 5 percent. When these governance problems are clustered, they account for the problems most often cited (23 percent). External political problems mentioned included exploitation by the United States, the Soviet Union, and other foreign powers (8 percent), and the conflict in Nicaragua (3 percent). Debt, unemployment, or poor economies were specifically mentioned by only 7 percent of the respondents. Human rights issues were mentioned in the context of Latin America by only two of the 1,246 individuals who were asked this question.[7] Drugs were not mentioned by any respondents (table 3).

Table 3. Latin America's Problems

"Thinking now specifically about Latin America, what do you think is the single biggest problem in the countries there?" Asked of the general population.

	Percentages
Bad leadership/unstable governments/civil wars	23
Poverty/hunger/malnutrition	21
Lack of know-how/education	8
Exploitation by other countries	8
Poor economies/unemployment/debt	7
Nicaragua conflict	3
Miscellaneous	11
Don't know	22
No answer	10

---

[7]Question asked of a split sample of the general population.

Those who perceived internal political problems to be very important in Latin America tended to be employed in professional or white-collar occupations. Respondents in the western United States and Hispanics were also somewhat more likely to perceive poor governance to be a problem in Latin America (table 4).[8]

One indication of Americans' general ignorance about developing countries in particular was the large share of respondents who were unable to name a single problem facing the regions of Latin America, Asia, and Africa. Roughly one-third did not offer any opinion in response to this question with respect to Asia (36 percent) or Latin America (32 percent). A significantly smaller number (11 percent) did not respond to the question in relation to Africa. This would seem to indicate that the 1984-1985 press coverage of Africa's food and development crisis had an impact on U.S. awareness of the continent.

The differentiation among regional development problems by the general public is most likely a result of the kind of information to which the public is exposed, primarily through the media. This is most clear in the case of Africa, but media coverage of other developing regions is probably similarly influential. For example, a study of U.S. press coverage of Mexico concluded that such coverage substantially changed in focus between 1983 and 1986. In 1986, "political coverage was heavily conditioned by episodes of electoral fraud in both 1985 and 1986, and by the greater attention paid by the U.S. media to the shortcomings of Mexico's political system." Moreover, although Mexico was in the midst of its second debt crisis in 1986, the study found that economic coverage of Mexico was substantially lower than in 1983.[9]

Most of the U.S. public has very negative perceptions of developing country governments as corrupt or incompetent and lay much of the blame for these countries' problems at the doors of their governments. Eighty-one percent of the public agreed (nearly one-half of them strongly) with the statement that: "Governments in Third World countries are largely to blame for creating their own problems through poor planning." When asked to rate a number of factors as responsible for improving conditions

---

[8]Caution should be used in interpreting all data on Hispanics, due to the small sample size.
[9]"U.S. Press Provides a New Picture," *Latin America Regional Reports, Mexico and the Caribbean*, RM-86-10, 4 December 1986.

Table 4. Latin America's Major Problem (Top Two Mentions)

"Thinking now specifically about Latin America, what do you think is the single biggest problem of the countries there?" Asked of the general population; results given in percentages.

	Total Sample	Bad Leadership/ Unstable Governments/ Civil Wars	Poverty
Total	100	23	16
Sex			
Men	48	24	23
Women	52	22	22
Age			
18-24	15	19	16
25-34	25	26	18
35-54	32	24	26
55 and over	26	22	27
Race			
White	84	23	22
Black	11	17	19
Hispanic*	2	37	17
Religion			
Catholic	24	22	24
Protestant	56	24	20
Income			
Under $15K	23	18	20
$15K-40K	48	24	22
Over $40K	21	22	27
Occupation of Chief Wage Earner			
Professional	37	28	27
White Collar	15	24	20
Blue Collar	35	19	17
Non-Working			
Retired	16	18	28
Homemakers	11	18	16
Education			
College Grad or More	24	32	28
Some College/ Technical School	24	19	27
High School or Less	49	20	16
Region			
West	17	29	21
North Central	28	22	24
Northeast	23	21	26
South	32	21	18
Political Identification			
Republican	30	26	21
Democrat	34	20	20
Independent	25	24	27

*Caution should be used in interpreting these data due to small sample size.

in the Third World, only 5 percent of the activist respondents gave Third World governments a great deal of credit, and 24 percent a fair amount of credit, for contributing to progress in their countries. A majority (64 percent) felt that Third World governments were either not at all or only slightly helpful.

Americans' Knowledge of the Third World

No analysis of public attitudes toward U.S.-Third World relations or development efforts can ignore the weakness of the American knowledge base on these questions, as demonstrated by the inability of large segments of the population to name a single development problem in Asia and Latin America. It is, however, important to remember that the public is generally uninformed about both domestic and foreign policy issues. This does not prevent the public from having strongly held opinions on subjects seen as important, such as taxes, the federal deficit, and nuclear arms control.

To measure the public's general level of knowledge on foreign policy issues, respondents to the general population survey were asked three factual questions: "Do you happen to recall whether the Reagan Administration is backing the Sandinistas or the Contras in Nicaragua?" "Do you recall which two nations took part in the SALT talks, now known as the START talks?" And, "Do you happen to recall whether the U.S. or the USSR is in NATO—that is, the North Atlantic Treaty Organization?" Approximately one-half of the respondents correctly answered each question, but less than one-third correctly answered at least two of the three questions.

"Well-informed" individuals—defined in this study as those who correctly answered at least two of the three factual questions—tended to be college-educated, upper-income, and in professional occupations. Men were more likely than women to fall into this category.

Among activists surveyed, 80 percent said the sentence "I don't know enough about Third World countries and their problems" described them very well or somewhat. This lack of knowledge did not necessarily reflect a lack of interest, however. Fifty-seven percent of the activists also said that the sentence "I'm not really that interested in Third World countries" described them "not at all," while only 10 percent said it described them very well and 32 percent said the phrase somewhat described them. The level of knowledge does appear to make a difference to U.S. opinion on Third World issues. For example, individuals defined in the general population survey as "well-informed" favored U.S. economic assistance more than the general public (63 percent, compared to 54 percent of the public as a whole). They were also more likely than the public as a whole to believe that the United States should give the Third World greater access to U.S. markets (46 percent, compared to 32 percent).

On issues that arguably relate more closely to values, however, individuals' information levels made less of a difference. For example, "well-informed" individuals did not differ from the general public in most frequently citing humanitarian feelings of concern or responsibility as their reasons for supporting U.S. economic aid. They were only slightly less likely than the general public (77 percent compared to 84 percent of the public as a whole) to agree with the statement, "We need to solve our own poverty problems in the United States before we turn attention to other countries."

AMERICAN ATTITUDES TOWARD U.S.-MEXICAN RELATIONS

The surveys for the ODC/InterAction study were conducted between April and September 1986. The survey of the general population was conducted between 7 April and 6 May, and the activist survey was carried out between 22 August and 2 September. These dates are important because of the extraordinary events in the binational relationship that occurred during that period. In mid-May, Senator Jesse Helms (R-NC), chairman of the Western Hemisphere Subcommittee, held hearings on U.S.-Mexican relations. At the hearings, Reagan administration officials accused Mexico of official corruption, narcotics trafficking, electoral fraud, and economic mismanagement. These public accusations on the part of U.S. officials, and the feuding within the administration that followed them, were headline news for several weeks around the United States. Although the general population survey was completed before the hearings began, the activists were interviewed roughly three months after they were completed, which may have influenced their opinions to some degree. The publicity surrounding the hearings was taken into consideration in designing the questionnaire: due to the highly public debate on Mexico's role in the U.S. drug problem, the drug issue was deliberately excluded from the questionnaire.

The U.S. Public's Knowledge of Mexico

The U.S. public is generally poorly informed about developing countries and their relations with the United States. It cannot
be demonstrated through the ODC/InterAction survey that there
is an exception in the case of Mexico, although the high incidence
of Americans traveling to Mexico does imply at least a certain
degree of familiarity with the country and its people relative to
other developing countries. This probably influences the perceptions of those who have traveled to Mexico about the people and
governments of that country, as well as its relationship with the
United States.

More Americans report visiting Mexico than any other developing country or region. Among the general public surveyed, 62
percent report having traveled outside of the United States and 30
percent specifically report having visited Mexico. Only Canada was
more frequently cited as a destination for foreign travel. Travel to
other developing countries was considerably lower (table 5). Older
and higher-income individuals also tended to have traveled to
Mexico more frequently than other groups (table 6).

Most travel to any foreign country was undertaken for pleasure
(70 percent), business (6 percent), or military service (21 percent).
Only 8 percent of all foreign travel was undertaken for educational
purposes, and only 2 percent involved working abroad. This implies
either short stays in foreign countries or exposure to somewhat

---

Table 5. Foreign Travel

Asked of the general population; results appear in percentages.

Have you ever traveled outside the United States	Yes	62

Which parts of the world have you ever visited?

	Of Those Ever Traveling	Of Total Population
Canada	69	43
Mexico	48	30
Western Europe	37	23
Caribbean	24	15
Eastern Europe	13	8
Asia	13	8
Far East	12	7
Central America	8	5
South America	8	5
Middle East	8	5
Africa	7	4
Other	2	1

Table 6. Americans Who Have Traveled to Mexico (percentages)

	Total Sample	Mexico Travelers
Total	100	100
Sex		
Men	48	55
Women	52	45
Age		
18-24	16	11
25-34	24	20
35-54	32	36
55 and over	27	33
Race		
White	84	88
Black	11	6
Hispanic*	2	4
Income		
Under $15K	25	17
$15K-$40K	47	45
Over $40K	19	29
Occupation of Chief Wage Earner		
Professional	35	44
White Collar	15	15
Blue Collar	36	25
Non-Working		
Retired	17	19
Homemakers	11	8
Education		
College Grad or More	24	36
Some College/ Technical School	24	28
High School or Less	50	34
Region		
West	16	27
North Central	29	25
Northeast	22	17
South	32	31

*Caution should be used in interpreting these data due to small sample size.

limited environments, such as military bases, resorts, and advanced urban areas.

Other recent surveys have provided some insight into the U.S. public's knowledge of Mexico. For example, a 1988 survey sponsored by the National Geographic Society discovered that eight out of ten respondents were able to locate Mexico on a map (more than double the number correctly identifying West Germany, Egypt, Vietnam, Sweden, or the Persian Gulf, and significantly more than were able to locate Central America, Japan, France, Italy, the United

Kingdom, or South Africa). In the same survey, however, only 15 percent correctly identified Mexico City as the world's most populated city.[10] In August 1988, just two months after the controversial and widely reported Mexican presidential election, a separate survey found that seven out of ten Americans had never heard of, or knew too little to form an opinion about, newly elected President Carlos Salinas de Gortari.[11]

Perceptions of the Importance of Mexico to the United States

Mexico is the United States' third largest trading partner and primary source of imported oil. The stagnant Mexican economy has increased the number of undocumented workers crossing the border. The collapse of the world oil market has threatened Mexico's ability to repay its foreign debt, and thus the stability of the U.S. banking system, and has resulted in depressed earnings for many U.S. corporations, a sharp fall in U.S. exports, and a slump in the U.S. border economy. Mexico has played a critical role in the Central American peace process, a high-priority issue on the U.S. policy agenda. The exchanges and movements across the 2,000 mile common border mean unprecedented cultural, social, and economic interchange between the two nations. In other words, Mexico is vital to U.S. national interests. Nonetheless, the ODC/ InterAction study found that only 40 percent of the public rated Mexico as very important to the United States (table 7).[12]

There were only slight differences on this issue according to income, profession, or education, although better-educated and higher-income individuals were somewhat more likely to rate

---

[10]Survey conducted by the Gallup Organization for the National Geographic Society, 30 April-8 May 1988

[11]Survey conducted by Marttila and Kiley for Americans Talk Security, 31 July-7 August 1988.

[12]Other surveys have shown, however, that the U.S. public does believe that Mexico is of vital interest to the United States. Of those surveyed in a 1986 Harris poll, 69 percent of the general public responded that it was very important "for the U.S. to have a stable, reliable, and friendly neighbor in the government of Mexico"; another 24 percent said it was somewhat important. (See Louis Harris,"Mexico Is Friendly But Has Serious Problems," Louis Harris, *Harris Survey,* 11 August 1986, Press Release No. 44.) More recently, 38 percent of those polled by the Daniel Yankelovich Group rated the economic problems of Mexico as an extremely serious or very serious threat to U.S. national security, while an additional 39 percent rated it as a somewhat serious threat (survey by Daniel Yankelovich Group for Americans Talk Security, 17-24 February 1988; data from the Roper Center for Public Opinion Research).

Table 7. Countries Rated "Very Important" to the United States

"Using our scale where 1 means not at all important and 10 means very important, please tell me how important you feel each of these countries is to the United States." Asked of the general population; results appear in percentages.

(Very important = ranking of 8, 9, or 10 in a scale of 1 to 10)

	Great Britain	Soviet Union	China	Mexico	Nigeria	India
Total	61	60	48	40	14	13
Sex						
Men	60	61	49	39	12	11
Women	61	59	45	42	16	15
Race						
White	64	62	48	42	12	13
Black	39	46	38	30	31	10
Hispanic*	57	57	60	43	20	23
Age						
18-24	53	51	48	22	13	10
25-34	58	67	48	35	13	11
35-54	65	64	52	47	16	15
55 and over	64	55	42	49	13	15
Religion						
Catholic	65	60	49	36	11	16
Protestant	61	59	44	43	16	12
Income						
Under $15K	52	52	42	39	17	18
$15K-$40K	63	60	47	40	13	12
Over $40K	66	74	57	43	9	8
Occupation of Chief Wage Earner						
Professional	61	68	55	44	12	10
White Collar	63	62	46	42	14	12
Blue Collar	60	53	43	36	16	16
Non-Working						
Retired	65	55	37	49	12	14
Homemakers	65	51	42	46	18	18
Education						
College Grad or More	58	75	55	45	11	10
Some College/ Tech. School	67	57	45	40	13	12
High School or Less	58	54	45	38	16	15
Region						
West	59	63	55	48	13	12
North Central	62	61	44	40	13	12
Northeast	64	62	53	37	14	16
South	58	56	42	40	16	12

*Caution should be used in interpreting these data due to small sample size.

Mexico as very important to the United States. Age also appears to play a factor in assessments of Mexico's importance. Older Americans tended to rate Mexico as very important more frequently. Americans living in the western United States tended to rate Mexico as very important more often than did those living in other regions. Even in the West, however, Mexico was generally perceived as less important than the Soviet Union, Great Britain, or China. Individuals in the general public with a history of activism[13] were slightly more likely to rank Mexico as very important to the United States—49 percent, compared to 40 percent of the public as a whole. Moreover, individuals rating Mexico as very important to the United States were somewhat more likely to be well-informed about foreign policy than the public at large (table 8).

While the general public did not accord Mexico the highest priority among the countries listed in the ODC/InterAction survey,

---

Table 8. Individuals Ranking Mexico "Very Important" to the United States

"Using our scale where 1 means not at all important and 10 means very important, please tell me how important you feel each of these countries is to the United States." Asked of the general population; results appear in percentages.

(Very important = ranking of 8, 9, or 10 in a scale of 1 to 10)

	Rating Mexico "Very Important"	Total Population
Total	40	100
Highly Active[a]	49	20
Awareness		
Poorly-Informed[b]	29	26
Well-Informed[c]	47	30
Third World Travel	46	45

[a]See footnote 13 for definition.
[b]Poorly-informed: individuals who incorrectly responded to all three of the factual questions on the general population questionnaire.
[c]Well-informed: individuals who correctly responded to at least two out of three of the factual questions on the general population questionnaire.

---

[13]This group is distinct from the "activists" surveyed. In the general population survey, 20 percent of the respondents were classified as "highly active" because they reported having ever undertaken six or more of the following activities: written a letter to the editor of a magazine or newspaper; written to or telephoned a radio or television station; written to an elected official; written something that was published (other than a letter to the editor); personally visited an elected official to express a point of view; addressed a public meeting; took an active part in some local civic issue; actively worked for a political party or candidate; engaged in fundraising; or worked actively as a volunteer in something nonpolitical.

activists clearly perceived Mexico as important to the United States. The activists in the ODC/InterAction study firmly rejected the suggestion that Mexico's economy has little impact on the U.S. economy. Seventy-seven percent disagreed with the statement, "Mexico's economic problems do not affect the U.S. economy very much" (table 9). Disagreement with this statement was found among all demographic subgroups, but better-educated, upper-income, and professional individuals tended to disagree more often than their counterparts.

Table 9. Mexico's Impact on the United States

"Mexico is the only Third World country bordering the United States. As I read you these statements about U.S.-Mexican relations, please tell me if you tend to agree or disagree with each one. Mexico's economic problems do not affect the U.S. economy very much." Asked of the activists; results appear in percentages.

	Agree	Disagree	Don't Know/ No Answer
Total	19	77	4
Sex			
Men	18	80	2
Women	20	74	6
Age			
Under 35	22	75	3
35-54	17	79	4
55 and over	18	76	6
Household Income			
Under $25K	22	72	6
$25K-$40K	17	78	5
Over $40K	17	81	2
Occupation			
Professional	15	83	2
White Collar	18	79	3
Blue Collar	24	73	3
Education			
College Grad or More	15	84	1
Some College/ Tech School	16	83	1
High School or Less	24	68	8
Political Identification			
Republican	15	82	3
Democrat	21	75	4
Independent	23	74	3
Region			
West	20	78	2
Northeast	19	80	1
North Central	16	79	5
South	23	70	7

There did appear to be a relationship between activists' perception that the Mexican economy is important to the United States and the perception of general economic linkages between the United States and the Third World. A subgroup was created of activists in the ODC/InterAction survey who appeared to recognize these linkages.[14] While 77 percent of the activists as a whole disagreed that the Mexican economy does not affect the U.S. very much, a slightly larger 86 percent majority of this specific subgroup disagreed (table 10).

Table 10. Views on U.S.-Mexican Relations of Those Who Perceive U.S.-Third World Economic Linkages[a]

Asked of activist respondents; results appear in percentages.

	Total	"Linkage Aware" Subgroup
"Mexico's economic problems do not affect the U.S. very much"		
Agree	19	12
Disagree	77	86
"The United States should exert political and economic pressure on Mexico to hold fair elections"		
Agree	54	59
Disagree	41	39
"Mexico should get priority over other needy nations for help from the U.S."		
Agree	52	59
Disagree	45	39

[a]See footnote 14 for definition.

Activists were more sharply divided on the issue of U.S. response to Mexican need. Fifty-two percent agreed and 45 percent disagreed that Mexico should be accorded priority over other needy countries for receiving U.S. help because of its geographic proximity (table 11). By 61-39 percent, a sizable majority of men

---

[14]These individuals agreed with at least two out of three statements concerning U.S.trade and debt policy. The statements were: "The United States should actively help reduce the foreign debt of Third World countries that face economic collapse"; "Americans should buy products from Third World countries because their prices are lower and it helps those countries get on their feet"; and "American banks should give Third World countries more financial credit and make it easier for them to repay their loans." Nineteen percent of the activist respondents qualified for this subgroup.

Table 11. Should Mexico Receive Priority Attention?

"As I read you these statements about U.S.-Mexican relations, please tell me if you tend to agree or disagree with each one. Because Mexico is our neighbor, it should get priority over other needy countries for help from the U.S." Asked of activists; results appear in percentages.

	Agree	Disagree	No Answer/ Don't Know
Total	52	45	3
Sex			
Men	61	39	*
Women	44	51	5
Age			
Under 35	42	55	3
35-54	57	41	2
55 and over	54	43	3
Household Income			
Under $25K	49	50	1
$25K-$40K	54	41	5
Over $40K	54	44	2
Occupation			
Professional	58	40	2
White Collar	49	46	5
Blue Collar	53	45	2
Education			
College Grad or More	55	42	3
Some College/ Tech School	54	42	4
High School or Less	47	50	3
Political Identification			
Republican	54	43	3
Democrat	56	43	1
Independent	50	45	5
Region			
West	47	50	3
Northeast	47	49	4
North Central	57	41	2
South	50	47	3

*Less than .5 percent

believe that Mexico should be accorded highest priority for U.S. assistance, while women disagreed 51-44 percent. Although a majority in all occupational categories favored helping Mexico first, those in professional occupations did so by the widest margin. Regionally, those in the West, Northeast, and South were divided on the issue, while those living in the north central states more frequently supported the idea of helping Mexico first.

Priority of Issues Affecting U.S.-Mexican Relations

The ODC/InterAction study specifically asked the general public to rank three issues in terms of their importance to U.S.-Mexican relations: Mexican immigration to the United States, political stability in Mexico, and the Mexican debt crisis. Immigration and political stability were found to vie for first place in U.S. public opinion. A slight plurality (35 percent) of the U.S. public considered Mexican immigration to the United States to be the most important issue affecting U.S.-Mexican relations, while just under one-third (32 percent) gave first place to Mexico's political stability. A smaller number (22 percent) considered Mexico's debt crisis to be the most important problem (table 12). This ranking of the three issues—immigration and political stability rated as more important than the debt crisis—was uniform across most demographic subgroups with only a few exceptions. By a small margin, college graduates tended to rank Mexico's debt crisis as the most important issue. Among "well-informed" Americans, the debt crisis emerged as the most important U.S.-Mexican issue (table 13).

Table 12. Most Important Issues Affecting U.S.-Mexican Relations

"Which of these do you think is the most important issue affecting our relationship with Mexico? And which is the second most important?" Asked of the general public; results appear in percentages.

	Most Important	Second Most Important
Immigration from Mexico to the United States	35	23
Political stability in Mexico	32	30
Mexico's debt crisis	22	32
Don't know	10	12
No answer	1	3

The roughly even division of opinion among issues is noteworthy. This could imply that all issues are basically perceived to be important or, conversely, that the public holds no firm opinion on any of the issues.

Among those who rated immigration as a more important U.S.-Mexican issue, blacks did so more often than either whites or Hispanics. Those in blue-collar occupations, with a high school education, or in lower-income households were also more likely to emphasize immigration. Americans in the western and southern states believed immigration to be the major problem somewhat more often than those in other parts of the country. Mexico's debt

Table 13. Most Important Issue Affecting U.S. Relationship with Mexico

Asked of the general population; results appear in percentages.

	Immigration from Mexico to U.S.	Political Stability in Mexico	Mexico's Debt Crisis	No Answer/ Don't Know
Total	35	32	22	11
Sex				
Men	33	31	28	8
Women	38	32	17	13
Race				
White	34	33	23	11
Black	46	23	16	15
Hispanic[a]	41	30	26	4
Age				
18-24	39	30	23	6
25-34	37	31	22	9
35-54	31	31	26	12
55 and over	36	34	17	13
Religion				
Catholic	35	31	23	10
Protestant	37	32	20	12
Income				
Under $15K	39	31	16	15
$15K-$40K	37	33	22	8
Over $40K	28	32	32	9
Occupation of Chief Wage Earner				
Professional	31	30	29	10
White Collar	34	35	22	10
Blue Collar	39	32	18	10
Non-Working				
Retired	39	36	14	10
Homemakers	40	39	8	13
Education				
College Grad or More	27	28	36	8
Some College/ Tech School	31	36	20	12
High School or Less	41	31	17	10
Region				
West	39	25	25	10
North Central	33	33	21	12
Northeast	31	35	26	8
South	39	32	18	12
Highly Active[b]	26	32	30	—
Well-Informed[c]	27	30	36	—

[a]Caution due to sample size.
[b]See footnote 13 for definition.
[c]Individuals who correctly responded to at least two out of three of the factual questions on the general population questionnaire.

crisis was more frequently identified as the most critical problem by men than by women. Respondents with incomes over $40 thousand a year were considerably more likely to select this response. Professionals and college graduates also tended to emphasize this problem. There were few demographic differences among those selecting Mexico's political stability as the major issue.

The high priority given to Mexican immigration to the United States is not surprising in light of the responses to other more general questions in the ODC/InterAction study concerning immigration and refugee policy. There is a striking degree of support among the general public for U.S. immigration restrictions to protect U.S. jobs. A large majority (71 percent) of the public agreed with the statement, "The United States should limit the number of immigrants entering the country because they compete with Americans for jobs." Forty-three percent agreed strongly with this view. Those who most often strongly agreed with this statement tended to live in lower-income households, and to be less educated (table 14). In contrast, there was a division among the general public as to whether or not the United States should open its borders to refugees. By a 55-42 percent majority, the public agreed that the United States should accept refugees fleeing from political oppression. A narrower 50-46 percent majority felt that the United States should accept refugees fleeing poverty, a category into which most immigrants from Mexico would fall.

At first glance, the public did not appear to make the distinction between political and economic refugees that guides official U.S. policy. However, closer examination of those who strongly agreed with the statements about admitting political and economic refugees shows that there was nearly twice as much strong support for accepting political refugees (21 percent) as for accepting economic refugees (11 percent). Strong support for political refugees was found in roughly one-fifth of all demographic subgroups, with better-educated individuals and those in professional households more likely to be strongly in favor. Strong agreement with accepting economic refugees was less widespread, with roughly one-tenth of all demographic subgroups agreeing (table 14).

Americans do seem to perceive a specific link between underdevelopment and U.S. immigration. Nearly two-thirds of the activists agreed with the statement, "Helping Third World countries become self-sufficient will cut down on the number of immigrants to the United States." This could indicate some recognition of the

Table 14. Views on U.S. Immigration Policy

"Do you tend to strongly agree, somewhat agree, somewhat disagree or strongly disagree with the following statements: (1) "The U.S. should limit the number of immigrants entering the country because they compete with Americans for jobs; (2) The U.S. should accept refugees fleeing poverty; and (3) The U.S. should accept refugees fleeing from political oppression?" Asked of the general public.

(Percent saying "Strongly Agree")

	U.S. Should Limit Immigrants	U.S. Should Accept Refugees Fleeing Poverty	U.S. Should Accept Refugees Fleeing Political Oppression
Total	43	11	21
Sex			
Men	42	12	19
Women	44	11	22
Age			
18-24	44	12	18
25-34	40	11	20
35-54	39	14	22
55 and over	50	9	22
Race			
White	42	10	21
Black	53	17	16
Hispanic*	40	27	22
Religion			
Catholic	44	12	22
Protestant	44	10	18
Income			
Under $15K	50	15	19
$15K-$40K	45	10	23
Over $40K	27	14	22
Occupation of Chief Wage Earner			
Professional	32	12	25
White Collar	44	11	24
Blue Collar	54	11	17
Non-Working			
Retired	49	10	23
Homemakers	49	13	17
Education			
College Grad or More	26	15	30
Some College/Tech School	36	8	23
High School or Less	56	11	16
Region			
West	35	14	23
North Central	48	9	21
Northeast	34	15	26
South	49	10	16

*Caution should be used in interpreting this data due to small sample size.

fact that the porous U.S.-Mexico border's function as a safety valve might decline were the Mexican economy to improve.

The relative lack of importance assigned to the debt crisis in U.S.-Mexican relations is consistent with responses to more general questions on debt in the ODC/InterAction study. Americans are not clearly supportive of U.S. efforts to help developing countries overcome the burdens of their debt problem, and the study found little evidence that they make any connection between the Third World's debt crisis and U.S. national interests or between the debt crisis and alleviating poverty in the developing world. For example, when asked to rate the importance of different kinds of U.S. aid programs for developing countries on a scale of one to ten, "giving money to Third World countries to pay their foreign debt" was ranked last by the public as a whole among fourteen different kinds of aid programs. Fifty-two percent of the public rejected the proposition that the United States "needs to do everything in its power to find solutions to the debt problems of Third World countries." Forty-six percent agreed with the statement, but only 14 percent agreed strongly (table 15).

Table 15. U.S. Debt Policy

"Do you tend to strongly agree, somewhat agree, somewhat disagree, or strongly disagree with the following statement: The U.S. needs to do everything in its power to find solutions to the debt problems of Third World countries." Asked of the general public; results appear in percentages.

	Strongly Agree	Somewhat Agree	Somewhat Disagree	Strongly Disagree
Total	14	33	30	22
Sex				
Men	17	34	29	19
Women	11	31	31	24
Age				
18-24	8	40	34	18
25-34	12	34	32	21
35-54	16	30	32	21
55 and over	15	31	22	26
Race				
White	13	33	30	21
Black	17	33	23	23
Hispanic*	13	23	37	23
Religion				
Catholic	15	30	30	23
Protestant	12	34	30	21

*Caution should be used in interpreting this data due to small sample size.

Continued on next page

Table 15. U.S. Debt Policy (Continued)

	Strongly Agree	Somewhat Agree	Somewhat Disagree	Strongly Disagree
Income				
Under $15K	12	32	29	23
$15K-$40K	15	31	30	22
Over $40K	13	39	29	20
Occupation of				
Chief Wage Earner				
Professional	16	32	31	20
White Collar	13	36	27	21
Blue Collar	11	32	31	24
Non-Working				
Retired	17	26	22	27
Homemakers	8	40	27	20
Education				
College Grad or More	17	36	27	18
Some College/				
Tech School	9	34	31	23
High School or Less	13	31	30	23
Region				
West	15	29	31	21
North Central	11	30	34	24
Northeast	15	37	29	17
South	15	34	25	24

*Caution should be used in interpreting this data due to small sample size.

A large majority (80 percent) of activists agreed that the United States should take care of its own financial problems before actively helping to reduce the foreign debt of economically unstable Third World countries (table 16). Upper-income, professional, and college-educated respondents, as well as those living in the western United States, were more likely to fall into the small minority (15 percent) that supported giving priority attention to reducing Third World debt. Two-thirds (66 percent) of the activists rejected the idea that U.S. banks should extend more credit to developing countries to help them repay their loans in favor of a statement that U.S. banks should not offer Third World countries better credit terms than they extend to U.S. companies (table 17). Those who favored giving the Third World more credit (27 percent) were somewhat more likely to be professionally employed and college educated.

The ODC/InterAction study did not focus on U.S. trade with Mexico. However, the responses to questions addressing U.S. trade policy issues with developing countries in general may be useful indicators of views on U.S.-Mexican trade.

Table 16. Deal with U.S. Financial Problems First?

"Which of these two statements do you tend to agree with more: The United States should actively help to reduce the foreign debt of Third World countries that face economic collapse; or The United States should take care of its own financial problems first?" Asked of activists; results appear in percentages.

	Help Reduce Debt	U.S. Problems First	Don't Know/ No Answer
Total	15	80	5
Sex			
Men	16	78	6
Women	13	82	5
Age			
Under 35	16	82	2
35-54	15	78	7
55 and over	13	81	6
Household Income			
Under $25K	10	86	4
$25K-$40K	14	80	6
Over $40K	21	72	7
Occupation of Chief Wage Earner			
Professional	23	68	9
White Collar	16	79	5
Blue Collar	11	85	4
Education			
College Grad or More	24	69	7
Some College/Tech School	11	83	6
High School or Less	8	88	4
Political Identification			
Republican	16	80	4
Democrat	18	76	6
Independent	11	82	7
Region			
West	21	74	5
Northeast	17	75	7
North Central	13	81	6
South	10	87	3

Strong protectionist sentiment surfaces on the issue of international trade: 60 percent of the general public said that the United States should restrict imports from the developing countries until the U.S. trade deficit is lowered, while 32 percent thought imports should be allowed and 8 percent were not sure. Only among college graduates did a small majority believe imports should be allowed (table 18).

Table 17. More Credit for the Third World?

"Which of these two statements do you tend to agree with more: American banks should give Third World countries more financial credit and make it easier for them to repay their loans; or Third World countries should not get better terms than any American company that borrows from the bank?" Asked of activists; results appear in percentages.

	More Credit	No Better Terms	Don't Know/ No Answer
Total	27	66	7
Sex			
Men	30	63	7
Women	25	68	7
Age			
Under 35	31	66	3
35-54	28	65	7
55 and over	24	65	11
Household Income			
Under $25K	26	68	6
$25K-$40K	25	67	8
Over $40K	33	61	6
Occupation of Chief Wage Earner			
Professional	34	58	8
White Collar	28	67	5
Blue Collar	23	73	4
Education			
College Grad or More	34	57	9
Some College/Tech School	25	69	6
High School or Less	23	71	6
Political Identification			
Republican	28	65	7
Democrat	31	62	7
Independent	26	67	7
Region			
West	29	61	10
Northeast	31	59	10
North Central	24	71	5
South	29	67	4

Activist respondents showed a similar protectionist tendency. When asked to choose between purchasing imported goods from Third World countries because "their prices are lower and it helps those countries get on their feet" and helping U.S. industries and workers by not buying Third World goods, 54 percent of the activists opted for the latter position. Only 31 percent favored purchasing imported goods, while 15 percent were undecided. Among the activists, as among the general public, those favoring purchasing imported goods were more likely to be male, better-educated, and to have incomes over $40,000 a year (table 19).

Table 18. U.S. Trade Policy

"Do you agree more that we should help Third World countries by letting them sell goods to the U.S., or more that the U.S. shouldn't allow so many foreign imports from the Third World until the U.S. trade deficit is lowered?" Asked of the general population; results appear in percentages.

	Should Help Sell	Shouldn't Allow	Don't Know
Total	32	60	8
Sex			
Men	39	56	5
Women	25	64	10
Age			
18-24	36	60	4
25-34	35	57	8
35-54	31	60	9
55 and over	26	63	10
Race			
White	31	60	9
Black	24	70	5
Religion			
Catholic	33	60	7
Protestant	28	62	10
Income			
Under $15K	26	66	7
$15K-$40K	32	60	8
Over $40K	41	52	7
Occupation of Chief Wage Earner			
Professional	41	51	8
White Collar	35	57	8
Blue Collar	23	69	8
Non-Working			
Retired	27	64	8
Homemakers	18	69	11
Education			
College Grad or More	51	42	7
Some College/Tech. School	33	58	9
High School or Less	21	70	8
Region			
West	43	50	7
North Central	30	61	8
Northeast	36	57	6
South	23	67	9

U.S. Policy toward Mexico's Elections

The activists surveyed were also divided on whether the United States should exert political and economic pressure on Mexico to hold fair elections. Fifty-four percent favored such pressure, but

Table 19. Should Americans Buy Third World Products?

"Which of these two statements do you tend to agree with more: Americans should buy products from Third World countries because their prices are lower and it helps those countries get on their feet; or to help U.S. industries and workers, Americans should not buy goods made in Third World countries even if they have to pay more for comparable American products." Asked of the activists; results appear in percentages.

	Should Buy	Should Not Buy	Don' Know/ No Answer
Total	31	54	15
Sex			
Men	39	45	16
Women	24	61	15
Age			
Under 35	27	57	16
35-54	34	50	16
55 and over	32	57	11
Household Income			
Under $25K	22	63	15
$25K-$40K	29	56	15
Over $40K	45	40	15
Occupation			
Professional	44	41	15
White Collar	30	54	16
Blue Collar	25	59	16
Education			
College Grad +	49	36	15
Some College/Tech School	23	63	14
High School or Less	20	64	16
Political Identification			
Republican	34	49	17
Democrat	30	58	12
Independent	30	53	17
Region			
West	38	46	16
Northeast	28	56	16
North Central	30	55	15
South	32	55	13

41 percent disagreed (table 20). Men were slightly more likely to favor U.S. pressure on this issue than women. Republicans favored such pressure by a 64-33 percent majority Democrats also favored pressure but by a smaller margin, and Independents were split on the issue. Individuals in the southern and western United States were nearly divided on the issue and those in the northeastern and north central states agreed by a heavier margin. On this issue, perhaps more than on any other addressed in the survey, the possible impact of the Helms' hearings in encouraging the perception

Table 20. U.S. Policy on Mexico's Elections

"As I read you these statements about U.S.-Mexican relations, please tell me if you tend to agree or disagree: The United States should exert political and economic pressure on Mexico to hold fair elections." Asked of the activists; results appear in percentages.

	Agree	Disagree	Don't Know/ No Answer
Total	54	41	5
Sex			
Men	59	38	3
Female	50	44	6
Age			
Under 35	50	44	6
35-54	57	41	2
55 and over	54	40	6
Household Income			
Under $25K	47	48	5
$25K-$40K	60	35	5
Over $40K	56	41	3
Occupation			
Professional	58	38	4
White Collar	52	45	3
Blue Collar	57	38	5
Education			
College Grad or More	52	44	4
Some College/ Tech School	61	37	2
High School or Less	53	42	5
Political Identification			
Republican	64	33	3
Democrat	54	43	3
Independent	48	47	5
Region			
West	49	41	10
North Central	56	41	3
Northeast	58	39	3
South	48	46	6

of the Mexican elections as corrupt should be borne in mind. The hearings also opened wide the possibility that overt U.S. pressure could and should be brought to bear to change the election situation, perhaps influencing activist opinion.

Support for a U.S. role in influencing the conduct of Mexican elections is consistent with the overall U.S. view of Third World governments as corrupt. It also falls in line with an overall public perception, revealed through other questions in the study, that it is in the U.S. interest to foster political reforms within developing countries. For example, three-quarters of the general population said that it is good policy for the United States to require a foreign government to carry out human rights reforms before it receives U.S. aid. Sixty-six percent also agreed that the United States should not give any kind of assistance to countries that do not have free elections or are ruled by dictators.

Despite public support for an active U.S. role in fostering political reforms in developing countries in general and Mexico in particular, it should be emphasized that the public is generally very cautious about potential over-involvement by the United States in Third World affairs. Among those in the general public who opposed U.S. military assistance to developing countries, 20 percent did so on the grounds that such assistance could lead the United States into war. Sixty-two percent of the general public agreed with the statement, "Aid programs get us too mixed up with other countries' affairs." Fifty-one percent agreed that "We should give the Third World countries less aid and leave them alone so they can develop in their own ways."

CONCLUSION

Americans are generally more familiar with Mexico, if only by virtue of business or vacation travel, than with any other country or region in the developing world. This is assumed to be a positive factor. Throughout the ODC/InterAction study, Third World travel was found to be a major factor influencing individuals' awareness of developing countries' problems and their degree of support for cooperative U.S. aid, trade, and finance policies toward the Third World. On the other hand, common sense tells us that the U.S. public is probably also familiar with Mexico through contacts of a less positive nature, such as media coverage of Mexico's role in the U.S. drug problem and personal or reported experiences of competition for employment with undocumented workers from Mexico. In this instance, one may wonder whether the kind of information the U.S. public receives about Mexico and U.S.-Mexican relations actually raises problems for those interested in building grassroots support for a more positive binational relationship.

A discouraging finding is that it is on precisely those issues which are vitally important in U.S.-Mexican relations—trade, debt, and immigration—which the U.S. public is the least likely to be sympathetic. In the case of international debt, both generally and in the case of Mexico specifically, neither the public nor the activists appear to be greatly aware of or concerned about the debt crisis, its relationship to U.S. or Mexican economic well-being, or its importance in terms of U.S. Mexican relations. Moreover, there does not appear to be widespread support for a strong U.S. role in resolving the problem.

In the case of more open trade and immigration, American perceptions are unambiguously hostile. On both issues the public sees actions that might assist Mexico, or contribute to the mutual economic well-being of the United States and Mexico over time, as being directly negative to the well-being of U.S. citizens and/or the U.S. economy. In all cases in the ODC/InterAction survey, these responses did not apply to Mexico specifically, but to the developing countries as a whole. Assuming that they do apply in the case of Mexico, however, they imply a tremendous need for education and/or advocacy on the part of those who would support binational trade and immigration policy reform.

Americans' desire to help other peoples and countries is largely grounded in feelings of humanitarian compassion, or a sense of individual or national responsibility. For those interested in building support for U.S. foreign assistance, such feelings may form a basis upon which constituencies can be built or strengthened. In the case of Mexico, however, this is more difficult. As an advanced developing country, Mexico does not need U.S. economic assistance. It needs the more open trade or financial policies which are critically important in the U.S.-Mexican relationship but either opposed or poorly understood by the majority of the U.S. public.

One problem facing those interested in building public support in the United States for a more positive U.S.-Mexican relationship is the extraordinarily negative perception the U.S. public has of developing-country governments in general. Assuming these negative impressions hold true in the case of Mexico—and there is no reason to believe that they do not—it will be difficult to stimulate support for a more mature and cooperative relationship with a government that is widely viewed as incompetent and corrupt.

One potential problem which the ODC/InterAction study did not examine is the extent to which the U.S. and Mexican publics may be aware of one another's problems but have their own conflicting interests or concerns. An unscientific poll conducted of its readers by the *Mexico City News* in late 1985 illustrates this point. A plurality of U.S. respondents (36 percent) cited drug trafficking as the top issue in the U.S.-Mexico relationship, while Central America topped the list among Mexican respondents, with 38 percent citing this issue. In response to another question in the same survey, 28 percent of the U.S. respondents favored a more closed common border, while no Mexican respondents favored such a policy.[15] While certain segments of U.S. and Mexican polity, such as the business and financial communities and the respective governments, may be increasingly aware of the commonality of U.S. and Mexican concerns, it is not at all clear whether the publics of either country have reached this point. Any effort to build or expand the constituency for bilateral initiatives would do well to start with groups which are already prone to be sympathetic. Those in the United States who are more aware of the importance of Mexico to the United States tend to be older, better educated, and more affluent, and to live in the western part of the country. They also tend to be relatively more informed about foreign policy issues, to be active in their communities, and to have traveled in the Third World.

A great deal more needs to be understood about U.S.-Mexican relations. Among the many issues that the ODC/InterAction study did not resolve or address are the degree and kind of knowledge that the U.S. public has about Mexico and U.S.-Mexican relations; the effect of that knowledge on the U.S. public's perceptions of the Mexican people, the Mexican government, and the bilateral relationship; and the extent to which the U.S. public's views on the U.S. trade or financial relationship with Mexico may differ from their views on U.S.-Third World economic relations more generally. The attitudes of certain key subgroups may also be of great interest, such as of Mexican-Americans, the U.S. business and financial community, congressional staffers and members of Congress, and other U.S. opinion leaders. A better understanding of the degree to which the opinions of the U.S. and Mexican publics may conflict or coincide on the full range of bilateral issues could also provide information valuable for building cross-border linkages among important audiences in both countries.

---

[15]"Poll: Readers Offer Views on Mexican-U.S. Relations,"the *Mexico City News*, 3 January 1986.

APPENDIX—SURVEY METHOD

InterAction and the Overseas Development Council commissioned Strategic Information Research Corporation (SIRC) to conduct the survey of the general population, the survey of activists, the focus group sessions, and the interviews with members of Congress and their aides. The design of the study and content of the various questionnaires were prepared by Director of Research Nancy Belden and her colleagues at SIRC—in consultation with InterAction and ODC representatives; Barry Sussman, special consultant to the Public Opinion Project; and members of the Survey Advisory Group.

GENERAL POPULATION SURVEY

The data for this portion of the research study were collected by means of telephone interviews with a representative sample of the adult population of the United States. In all, 2,427 interviews were conducted. This unusually large sample size permitted close analysis of certain demographic groups.

Sample Design. The frame for this sample was all adults eighteen years of age and older living in the United States. The sample was a random probability sample, based on all telephone-equipped households in the United States

To ensure that every household with a telephone in the country had an equal chance of being included in the sample, a random-digit-dialing (RDD) technique was utilized, which selected telephone numbers at random from all potentially available telephone numbers in the United States.

Interviewing. The questionnaire used in this study was separated into two versions. This split sample method—meaning certain questions were asked of only half the sample—made possible the inclusion of more questions on a wider array of topics. The questionnaire was field-tested prior to final approval by ODC representatives. The fieldwork took place at the National Telephone Research Center from 7 April to 6 May 1986.

All interviewing was monitored from a central control booth by an interviewing supervisor, who was responsible for validating questionnaire responses. Interviews were administered during the evening and on weekends, when the incidence of adults at home has been found to be highest. Once a household was reached, the respondent was selected at random from the adult residents living there, according to the sampling plan. If the respondent was not available, as many as three later attempts were made to call the selected respondent.

During the interviewing process, the sample was monitored to ensure that the appropriate proportion of respondents was represented according to sex and geographical area.

Weighting. The data were weighted by race and age to correspond to U.S. census estimates.

Margin of Error. Version 1 of the questionnaire was administered to 1,218 adults and Version 2 to 1,209 adults. For results based on samples of this size, one can say with 95 percent confidence that the error due to sampling and other random effects could be plus or minus 2.8 percentage points. For results based on the combined sample of 2,427 adults, the margin of error at the 95 percent confidence level is plus or minus 2.0 percentage points. The margin of error for subgroups discussed in the text is correspondingly larger.

ACTIVIST SURVEY

Data for this portion of the research were collected by means of telephone interviews with 502 American adults who met the criteria for "activism" as outlined below.

Sample Design. The sample of activist respondents was drawn from Simmons Market Research Bureau's (SMRB) comprehensive national database, the 1985 Study of Media and Markets. This study is the result of personal interviews on consumption and purchasing patterns with a national probability sample of U.S. adults (eighteen years and older) in nineteen thousand different households.

Using the Simmons survey as a sample frame, potential respondents were selected on the basis of ever having done two or more of the following activities:

• written to the editor of a magazine or newspaper;
• written to or telephoned a radio or television station;
• written to a public official about some matter of public business;
• written something that has been published;

- personally visited a public official to express a point of view;
- addressed a public meeting;
- taken an active part in some local civic issue;
- engaged in fund raising; and
- actively worked as a non-political volunteer.

The mean number of activities undertaken by the respondents to the InterAction/ODC activist survey was 2.5.

Interviewing. Telephone interviewing was conducted by Marketing, Inc., a nationwide WATS telephone center located in Long Island, New York, from 22 August to 2 September 1986. Trained interviewers, working under the close supervision of Marketing, Inc. professionals, conducted the interviews in the early evening hours. A total of 502 telephone interviews were completed. All respondents were individuals previously interviewed by SMRB and had been selected as part of a random probability sample of Americans.

Margin of Error. For results based on a sample of 502, one can say with 95 percent confidence that the error due to sampling and other random effects could be plus or minus 4.4 percentage points.

3

Mexico in the U.S. Media, 1979-88: Implications for the Bilateral Relation

John Bailey

In an era of mass politics, an important aspect of international relations concerns the images that citizens of different countries hold about one another. The communications media are probably the most significant single source of information that influence such images. In turn, these impressions affect behavior with respect to both concrete and intangible acts. They affect, for example, travel or investment as well as statements of attitudes. Taken together, the images, acts, and attitudes constitute a kind of mobilized bias, which—when positive—can facilitate international cooperation. When negative, such a bias can complicate relations.

Mexico and the United States, bound by geography and history but divided by unequal wealth, power, and distinctive variants of Western culture, have experienced periods of friction as well as of relative harmony. Between World War II and the late 1960s bilateral relations were generally managed in a normal, business-like manner. Reasons for this include both international and domestic factors. The relative stability of a bipolar world in the postwar period provided clear rules of the game: the United States

Revised and updated version of "México en los medios de comunicación estadunidenses: inferencias para la relación bilateral," in *México—Estados Unidos, 1986*, ed. Gerardo Bueno (México: El Colegio de México, 1987), pp. 125-56. Alon Pinkas and Fred Shepherd helped gather data. Michael Robinson, Leopoldo Gómez, Leonardo Ffrench, and Vincent Hovenac made useful comments. The usual disclaimers apply.

took the lead in the "high politics" of strategic global questions, and Mexico followed. Domestically, both the United States and Mexico achieved relatively high levels of internal political consensus on major issues, including foreign policy. The consolidation of the Mexican political system during the 1940s and 1950s reinforced adherence to a defensive foreign policy based on widely accepted principles, with historical roots that could be traced to the mid-nineteenth century. The U.S. preoccupation with global issues permitted flexibility, with a clear emphasis on stability, in its dealings with Mexico. Both countries sought to insulate the bilateral relation from broader regional and global issues.

Since the late 1960s, however, the foundations for a "normal" bilateral relation have begun to erode. The international order entered a more volatile period with détente, the rise of the European Economic Community and Japan, and the enhanced status of the newly industrializing powers. At roughly the same time, Mexico's import-substitution industrialization development strategy encountered a series of obstacles to continued growth; pressures continued to mount for reform, however defined. As part of a more general effort to promote change, President Luis Echeverría shifted emphases in both domestic and foreign policies in the early 1970s, and Mexico pursued a more active role in regional issues and in the North-South dialogue. At roughly the same time the United States encountered setbacks to its status as the world's preeminent economic and military power. Its internal politics as well reflected greater volatility as the New Deal Coalition continued to unravel. The postwar bipartisan consensus on foreign policy also faltered. These trends spilled over into the bilateral relation, generating several incidents that signalled increased tensions.[1]

The bilateral relation suffered new strains, beginning in the mid-1970s, such as the 1973 oil shock, disagreements in 1977 over petroleum and gas policies, and differing perspectives on the civil wars in Central America, narcotics trafficking, and external debt. These new issues in turn complicated more manageable points of dispute such as illegal migration, fishing, international boundaries, and the myriad problems inherent in a shared 2,000-mile border.

---

[1]This comment on the bilateral relation follows the framework set out by Carlos Rico, "Las relaciones México-Estados Unidos en 1985: antecedentes y evolución posible del conflicto," (Mexico: Instituto Latinoamericano de Estudios Transnacionales, 1986). Dramatic incidents during the early 1970s include "Operation Intercept," which closed the U.S.-Mexico border for brief time, and a temporary 10 percent surcharge placed by the United States on all imports.

Cast adrift from the moorings of the 1940-70 period, the internal politics of both Mexico and the United States have become both more conflictive and more important to the bilateral relation. Mexico embarked upon a profound, lengthy, and difficult transition in the mid-1980s. The United States confronts a crisis of its own, albeit with symptoms—bloated debt, trade and fiscal deficits, increasingly skewed income distribution, and drug abuse—that are still less immediately destabilizing than those of Mexico. In addition, and quite apart from intergovernmental relations, the two countries are growing increasingly integrated in economic, social, and cultural terms, most visibly in the border region. This general setting leads to more points of irritation between the United States and Mexico, and bilateral issues resonate more loudly in each country's internal politics.

The mass media of both countries reflect and reinforce the strains in the bilateral relation. But in this respect, as in many others, the relation is asymmetrical. Mexicans are more attentive to their image in the U.S. media than vice versa, and they were troubled by what they saw and heard after 1981. In the view of many, the news coverage tended to be unbalanced, superficial, and overwhelmingly negative. Quite understandably, some Mexicans— private citizens and government officials alike—entertained deep suspicions that Mexico had become the target of a massive disinformation campaign orchestrated by certain forces (U.S. government, investors, or ideological conservatives) to extract some concession (on policy toward Central America, or on trade and investment). Too often, U.S. observers dismiss Mexican complaints as an expression of unfounded (and ingrained) xenophobia or as an erroneous projection of the Mexican system—where the media are indeed more closely controlled—onto the United States.[2]

ARGUMENTS AND DATA SOURCES

This chapter reports the coverage of Mexico by two U.S. newspapers and three national television networks for the decade 1979-1988 and speculates about how the coverage affects the bilateral

[2]See Alan Riding, *Distant Neighbors: A Portrait of the Mexicans* (New York: Knopf, 1985), pp. 316-23. For example, "after the first of several devaluations of the Mexican peso in 1982, the [Mexican] officials became convinced that the State Department was responsible for a series of television reports and newspaper articles questioning Mexico's political stability" (p. 323). See the speech by Manuel Camacho, "En defensa de México," given in Washington, D.C., on 12 November 1986, and reprinted in *México-EAU: cooperación y conflicto* (memoria del foro efectuado en México, D.F., del 15 al 18 de diciembre de 1986), pp. 11-17.

relationship. The dailies are the *New York Times* and the *Washington Post,* and the networks are ABC, CBS, and NBC. The *Times* and *Post* were chosen from the nearly seventeen hundred dailies in the United States because they, along with the *Wall Street Journal* and the *Christian Science Monitor* and a select few regional papers such as the *Los Angeles Times,* head up the so-called prestige press. The prestige papers are important in several respects. They provide wire services and syndicated columns to newspapers throughout the country, and U.S. social and political elites typically read one or more on a consistent basis. The press influences electronic media because broadcast journalists comb the papers for news stories and leads. Television is the principal source of foreign news for most U.S. citizens, and though they are slipping somewhat in ratings, the evening network news programs are still dominant. Prestige dailies, especially the *New York Times,* and television network news programs are monitored by Mexican elites. Nineteen seventy-nine was chosen as a beginning point to facilitate building on previous research.

Strictly considered, the data report quantities of coverage and not quality. Given my own sampling and the comments of others, however, I believe I can infer something about the likely tone of the coverage from the timing and nature of the reported events. Also, I assume that media coverage influences elite opinion in a predictable manner, such that an increase in quantity of news, most of it negative, worsens the image of the subject.

I shall attempt to show that U.S. media attention to Mexico increased substantially in 1985 and 1986 and that concerns about inadequate, superficial, and unbalanced reporting have considerable basis in fact. Coverage increased again in 1988 but this time in a less critical vein. While the different media appear to act in unison, complaints about news campaigns designed to destabilize Mexico are both mistaken and dangerous. They are mistaken because the U.S. media operate according to their own internal logic, with considerable independence from other forces. Further, complaints about a conspiracy are dangerous because they reinforce negative behavior that can worsen the bilateral relationship in unnecessary ways. A policy prescription implied by this analysis is that Mexicans have the option to influence the U.S. media, and such would constitute a more positive response.

Several events caused media coverage of Mexico to vary markedly in the period from 1979 to 1986. The 1979 oil shock and U.S.

concern with energy sources reinforced interest in Mexico. The explosion of the Central American crisis, also in 1979, added two more themes: Mexico as the ultimate domino, whose fall would bring chaos to the U.S. border, and Mexico's Central American policy, which often differed from that of the U.S. government. The election of Ronald Reagan reinforced coverage. His experience as governor of California put him in closer touch with Mexico, and his campaign rhetoric about a North American Accord suggested special interest in the United States' contiguous neighbors. Also, Reagan's hard-line, anti-Soviet view of foreign relations was reflected in an East-West optic on Central American issues, with greater potential for conflict with Mexico. Mexico's August 1982 collapse brought into clearer relief the enormity of the debt situation, if not of the structural economic crisis that helped cause it. But for the media the key years by far were 1985 and 1986, beginning with political violence along the border and the sensational murder of a U.S. Drug Enforcement Administration (DEA) agent and his pilot in the state of Jalisco, followed in rapid succession by drug scandals, electoral fraud, devastating earthquakes, and an oil price slump that reintensified the debt crisis.

Stimulated in part by hearings in the U.S. Senate, much of the ample media coverage in 1986 reworked the themes and stories of the previous year. Then, precisely as a bilateral summit was focusing attention on Mexico, another DEA agent was detained and beaten by police in Guadalajara. This was followed by still more allegations of electoral fraud, again in Chihuahua, which heightened attention to the related problems of economic crisis and illegal migration.

A valley of relative calm in 1987 followed the peaks of 1985 and 1986. The 1988 presidential election in Mexico generated considerable attention in the U.S. media, however, although it is too early to tell whether this represents a short-term "bump" or the beginning of a sustained increase.

After reviewing the data on coverage, I speculate about the likely implications for bilateral relations. Although the data are inadequate, it appears that by mid-1987 Mexico's overall image in the United States had not been hurt substantially by media attention, at least as measured by two public opinion polls. The polls do show a significant shift in U.S. opinion about Mexico as a stable ally, however, and a marked decline in those holding a "very favorable" opinion of that country. By late 1986 the image of the

U.S. government and population held by Mexicans also may have deteriorated somewhat. Overall, the opinion data are too scanty to support firm conclusions. The more significant implication is that through a variety of feedback and amplifying mechanisms, U.S. media attention on Mexico complicated internal Mexican politics at a critical time. As the two neighbors attempt to accommodate themselves to a changed bilateral and global setting, one can expect future episodes of conflict to be amplified by the media. Especially important is the beginning of a new political situation in Mexico marked by the 1988 elections.

U.S. MEDIA COVERAGE OF MEXICO, 1979-1988

An introductory note on the nature of the U.S. media, even grossly simplified, is useful to gain perspective on the recent treatment of Mexico. The media are hardly neutral in their reporting, and it is unrealistic to expect unbiased coverage by any media anywhere: the very act of selecting topics for coverage implies biases. Further, the media's underlying values act with even greater force in interpreting foreign affairs. They are ethnocentric in the sense of judging foreign countries by mainstream U.S. values and in emphasizing items that concern U.S. citizens and interests.[3] The media hold a liberal pluralist conception of democracy, one which stresses individual freedoms and competition among parties in clean elections. Furthermore, they support a moderate form of benign capitalism, regulated by government to prevent abuses of monopoly and exploitation. Newsmen typically see themselves as the guardians of public morality and social order, alert to expose the misbehavior of public officials or others who hold offices of public trust in such areas as banking, religion, or education.[4]

These values form a rudimentary ideology, a mixture of liberal (in both classical and New Deal senses) and conservative views.

[3]Ethnocentrism holds, of course, for Mexico as well. Though I know of no specific study on this topic, I would hypothesize that the United States receives a significantly more negative treatment in the Mexican print media than does Mexico in the United States. Electronic media in Mexico, especially the television stations owned and operated by Televisa, probably cast the United States in a more favorable light. See Daniel Levy, "The Political Consequences of Changing Socialization Patterns," in *Mexico's Political Stability: The Next Five Years*, ed. Roderic A. Camp (Boulder, Colo.: Westview, 1986), pp. 19-46.
[4]This paragraph and the one following draw on Herbert J. Gans, *Deciding What's News: A Study of CBS Evening News, NBC Nightly News, Newsweek and Time* (New York: Pantheon, 1979).

The more basic value, though, is a reformism much like Progressivism—an essentially urban, middle-class, reformist movement of the early twentieth century, in which journalists played important roles. These are media that favor open, meritocratic government and oppose populism, socialism, communism, and all forms of corruption. One might argue as well that they are conservative, in the sense of preserving a social order based for the most part on U.S. middle- and upper-class values.

The dynamics of reporting often produce a phenomenon known as "pack journalism," which can sometimes appear as an orchestrated campaign on one or another topic, appearing to the victim or skeptical viewer as a conspiracy. In vulgar form a conspiracy view might hold that economic elites control both government and media, to the extent that, for example, individual bankers or industrialists—either directly or through elected puppets—can simply telephone instructions to editors or producers. There may be one-company towns in the United States where the reality might approach this stereotype, but at the regional and national levels the relationships are more complex and dynamic.

As sketched in figure 1, both the media and politicians are constantly monitoring society and social elites as well as each other. The relationship is one of cooperation and conflict. Journalists need access to sources, and politicians seek favorable media treatment. Politicians, therefore, along with many other elites and interests, work to influence media behavior. Since politicians are considered newsworthy, the media typically cover their activities. Major politicians make statements that are duly reported in the prestige press and thence magnified through wire services and the electronic media "echo." An important factor in this dynamic is the concern among journalists, newspapers, and broadcast stations—as professional business enterprises—of losing out to competitors. Thus, the sequence of statement, coverage, amplification and reaction can give the impression of an orchestrated campaign.

Figure 1. Key Relationships in Media Behavior

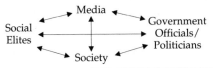

The dynamic of reporting, however, is shaped by several factors. First, the media filter and evaluate news by judging the motives and accuracy of the sources. A politician thus might receive "straight" coverage for a statement and then be subjected to a chorus of criticism by critics and commentators about motives and accuracy. Second, politicians are attentive to broader social concerns and so cloak their messages in symbols that will influence society. One implication of this is that politicians find it difficult to sponsor projects that are irrelevant to societal interests, or to advocate points of view that are antagonistic to mainstream beliefs. A politician of presidential stature might enjoy greater latitude to choose issues, but even a president as popular as Ronald Reagan can encounter resistance to his policies (as opposed to his personal acceptance).[5] Also, the pace of breaking stories means that the media's attention span is variable: what might appear as a major and enduring topic—the Central American wars serve as a good example—may dominate the news for three or four days, only to recede to the back pages or disappear altogether as the media shift their attention to something else. Finally, recent research suggests that "the overwhelming majority of the general public believes most of what it hears, sees, or reads in the nation's press," and that "perceived believability of the news media is *not* closely related to those political and demographic variables that typically divide public opinion in America."[6] The media thus have a large stake in preserving their credibility.

All of these considerations suggest that it would be difficult to invent and sustain a media campaign. When certain conditions converge, however, the result may be a burst of intensive coverage that indeed appears as a campaign. The key conditions are one or more spectacular incidents that touch on deeply felt societal concerns that may in turn be magnified by politicians. Recent examples of such convergences include the 1985 hostage incidents in Europe and the 1986 Challenger space disaster.

---

[5]Polls consistently reveal a gap in public support between President Reagan as a personality and the policies he supports. This gap is especially apparent in foreign policy, for example, toward Central America.
[6]Michael J. Robinson and Andrew Kohut, "Believability and the Press," *Public Opinion Quarterly* 52 (1988): 174.

The bulk of U.S. reporting concerns domestic matters. With respect to quantities of international content of newspapers, a study of four major dailies during 1972-1978 found greatest consistent attention to the USSR, China, Japan, and the principal European countries and variable attention to trouble spots (e.g., the Middle East), with considerably less emphasis on developing countries. Even so, Mexico received consistent space from the *Chicago Tribune* and the *Los Angeles Times*. The *New York Times* and the *Washington Post* devoted greater coverage to Europe than to other regions, "but both granted Mexico priority among Third World states and 'countries south of the Rio Grande.' All else being equal, events elsewhere in Latin America, Africa, and Asia received less attention than Mexican affairs."[7]

As of the late 1970s, more than two-thirds of the U.S. population cited television as their principal source of news, up from 60 percent in 1971. Satellite communications and electronic newsgathering equipment have dramatically enhanced foreign news coverage. During the 1970s, the average network news program contained seventeen stories with a mean level of 37 percent international news content. With about ten of twenty-seven minutes of a typical newscast devoted to international events, only brief treatments of a few countries can be aired. Only about twenty nations were mentioned in more than 2 percent of the international news stories. As in the newspapers, these tended to be major powers (the USSR, Great Britain, France, West Germany, Japan, China) or countries engaged in major conflicts (Vietnam, countries of the Middle East). Coverage of developing countries was relatively slighted. Attention to Latin America by the networks showed a gradual increase over the period from 1972 to 1979 and, with the exception of Mexico, coverage of most countries in the region came in response to crises.[8]

A study of network news coverage of Latin America during 1970-73, 1978-79 found relatively greater attention to Mexico and Cuba and stressed television's focus on crises.

---

[7]T.M. Laichas, "Mexico in the U.S. Press: A Quantitative Study, 1972-1978," *Statistical Abstract of Latin America* 20 (1980): 586-87.

[8]James F. Larson, "International Affairs Coverage on U.S. Evening Network News, 1972-1979," in *Television Coverage of International Affairs*, ed. William C. Adams (Norwood, N.J.: ABLEX, 1982), pp. 15-44. *Time*, 16 March 1987, p. 63, reported that "in 1980 the three [network news] broadcasts attracted 72 percent of viewers; so far this season the proportion is 63 percent."

While the coverage on Mexico and Cuba is also time and issue determined, of all the Latin American nations, these two countries received the most consistent network attention over time and, relatively speaking, over a mix of issues. The pattern of issues is the most balanced for Mexico in that a wide variety of issues tended to be covered in any one year. This pattern suggests that geographical proximity and the interdependence of problems may encourage, however weakly, more consistent and multifaceted coverage.[9]

By and large, television attention to Latin America increased during the period from 1972 to 1979, jumping from 6.6 to 14.1 percent of network news foreign coverage.[10] As might be expected, Cuba and Central America figured prominently in the increase. Mexico, which consistently ranked among those most covered, rose from seventeen minutes of network coverage in 1970 to eighty-eight minutes in 1979.[11]

Turning to more recent trends, table 1 reports media coverage of Mexico during 1979-1988. The data show a peak in 1979, a minor increase in 1982, a pronounced resurgence in 1985 and 1986, and possibly the beginnings of another in 1988. Consistent with the trend of the 1970s, the *Times* averaged more space on Mexico than the *Post*, although the *Post* "caught up" in 1985-1986. Of the three television networks on the whole, NBC and CBS paid the most attention to Mexico, although ABC almost closed the gap in 1985.

Each news organization registered spots of special activities, but generally heightened coverage appears in five clusters. Much happened in 1979, the first quarter of which combined visits to Mexico by President Jimmy Carter and Pope John Paul with interest in energy issues caused by the second oil shock. Later that same year came a cabinet shake-up, visits by Fidel Castro and the Shah of Iran, the blowout of an oil well in the Gulf of Mexico, midterm elections in Mexico, immigration legislation in the United States,

---

[9]Waltraud Queiser Morales, "Revolutions, Earthquakes and Latin America: The Networks Look at Allende's Chile and Somoza's Nicaragua," in Adams, *Television Coverage of International Affairs*, p. 89.
[10]Larson, "International Affairs Coverage on U.S. Evening Network News," p. 37.
[11]Morales, "Revolutions, Earthquakes and Latin America," p. 82.

and the deepening crisis in Central America. After 1979 the pace of coverage declined appreciably until Mexico's financial collapse and bank nationalization in the third quarter of 1982.

Table 1. News Coverage of Mexico in the United States, 1979-1986 (by calendar quarter, in column inches or seconds of evening network news)

		NYT	WP	ABC	CBS	NBC	Total
1979	1	1285	614	1700	1865	1950	7414
	2	478	133	230	480	180	1501
	3	604	482	940	350	140	2516
	4	371	264	705	360	750	2450
1980	1	314	109	—	150	550	1123
	2	267	65	140	150	190	812
	3	210	80	140	55	110	595
	4	160	61	180	260	560	1221
1981	1	198	231	790	510	510	2239
	2	139	240	320	560	920	2179
	3	227	147	480	1020	990	2864
	4	275	119	—	170	150	614
1982	1	224	99	640	1140	1300	3403
	2	267	42	300	280	160	1049
	3	500	282	1160	1860	1050	4852
	4	572	91	330	140	400	1533
1983	1	175	128	450	880	660	2293
	2	160	127	50	150	220	707
	3	281	198	780	660	450	2369
	4	77	84	190	680	70	1101
1984	1	292	72	50	600	250	1264
	2	281	215	700	590	360	2146
	3	257	204	340	190	1000	1991
	4	276	149	380	920	880	2605
1985	1	242	332	2040	1900	1390	5904
	2	218	311	290	610	440	1869
	3	421	376	2680	2810	3490	9777
	4	235	284	510	710	1020	2759
1986	1	408	180	270	580	680	2118
	2	856	863	1640	1530	1770	6659
	3	479	532	1200	2490	1430	6131
	4	874	255	510	300	100	2039
1987	1	287	305	90	130	380	1192
	2	378	117	230	210	170	1105
	3	371	288	390	500	720	2209
	4	348	141	550	200	150	1389
1988	1	436	79	480	260	900	2155
	2	405	187	320	530	370	1812
	3*	628	512	410	840	310	2700

* July 1988 only (NYT = *New York Times*; WP = *Washington Post*; ABC = American Broadcasting Company; NBC = National Broadcasting Company; CBS = Columbia Broadcasting System)

Nineteen eighty-five, like 1979, was an extraordinary year. On 11 February, Enrique Camarena, a DEA agent assigned to Guadalajara, and Alfredo Zavala, his pilot, were reported missing. Some three weeks later their bodies were found, bearing signs of torture, and a grisly saga of drug-related violence, corruption, and official incompetence unfolded. In June and July the U.S. media focused on Mexico's midterm elections, emphasizing allegations of fraud in the northern states of Sonora and Nuevo León. Devastating earthquakes struck in September, and finally, in November, oil prices softened and attention shifted to the debt issue.

The main stories in 1986 dealt with the implications of the oil price collapse for Mexico's economy and capacity to pay interest on its external debt. In May Senator Jesse Helms (R-NC) chaired hearings on Mexico that emphasized problems of drugs, illegal migration, corruption, and political authoritarianism. The hearings generated considerable attention and contributed to a recycling of the themes and events of 1985. Then on 18 August 1986, just two days after presidents Miguel de la Madrid and Ronald Reagan met in Washington, the networks broke the news that Mexican police in Guadalajara had apprehended and beaten a DEA agent. This incident, combined with renewed allegations of electoral fraud and further deterioration of the Mexican economy, generated yet another round of negative coverage. Media attention to Mexico declined in volume and moderated in tone in 1987 for a variety of reasons. Coverage in 1988 focused largely on the presidential elections, to be discussed in a later section.

The *New York Times* shows few exceptions to the general pattern (table 2).[12] The bulk of its coverage focused on political and economic subjects, with peaks of coverage in 1979, 1982, and 1986. It paid considerable attention to immigration issues in 1979 and 1984, when immigration legislation was under consideration in the United States. Its reaction to the drug-related murders in 1985 was relatively muted in comparison with the *Post* and the television

---

[12]A word on method. The categories used here are adaptations of those reported by Morales, "Revolutions, Earthquakes and Latin America," p. 85. The Information Service for Latin America publishes complete clippings from several U.S. and one British paper during 1979-1986. It includes news stories, editorials, and letters to the editor. I regard column inches as more useful than stories as the unit of analysis. My assistants assigned each item to only one category, with the story title especially important in the assignment. Measurements were done in whole numbers of column inches from beginning to end of text.

networks. There was an especially pronounced surge in attention to political, economic, and drug-related issues in 1986.

Table 2. *New York Times* Coverage of Mexico, 1979-1988 (by calendar quarter, in column inches)

		Pol	Eco	Dis	Dru	Cor	Imm	Vio	Oth	Total	
1979	1	363	504	—	—	114	224	00	80	1285	
	2	77	221	—	33	—	56	—	91	478	
	3	140	199	18	30	—	146	5	66	604	
	4	87	160	25	—	25	50	24	00	371	(2738)
1980	1	80	142	—	41	12	—	—	39	314	
	2	92	88	—	13	13	34	—	27	267	
	3	97	101	—	—	12	—	—	—	210	
	4	38	48	—	—	20	18	—	36	160	(951)
1981	1	135	59	—	—	—	—	4	—	198	
	2	56	72	27	—	—	—	1	8	139	
	3	70	113	—	—	—	3	2	39	227	
	4	138	65	8	—	—	15	—	49	275	(839)
1982	1	93	100	—	—	—	—	—	31	224	
	2	99	141	2	—	—	—	25	—	267	
	3	81	393	—	19	7	—	—	—	500	
	4	209	257	—	—	42	64	—	—	572	(1563)
1983	1	21	93	—	—	33	28	—	—	175	
	2	126	14	—	—	—	11	—	9	160	
	3	68	76	—	—	44	12	12	69	281	
	4	41	36	—	—	—	—	—	—	77	(693)
1984	1	48	94	—	10	55	9	—	76	292	
	2	202	41	—	—	—	34	4	—	281	
	3	64	128	2	—	—	27	20	16	257	
	4	95	92	24	—	—	34	13	18	276	(1106)
1985	1	48	63	4	53	—	—	—	74	242	
	2	105	21	—	17	14	—	18	43	218	
	3	84	84	163	3	—	26	21	40	421	
	4	57	75	62	16	—	—	3	22	235	(919)
1986	1	9	299	10	16	—	26	22	26	408	
	2	244	287	12	275	15	—	—	23	856	
	3	161	145	2	90	16	14	3	48	479	
	4	225	252	22	101	91	158	—	25	874	(2617)
1987	1	37	100	—	16	38	41	14	41	287	
	2	18	152	—	31	25	102	—	50	378	
	3	104	96	8	40	24	67	—	32	371	
	4	112	236	—	—	—	—	—	—	348	(1384)
1988	1	233	166	4	26	—	33	—	24	436	
	2	158	73	—	74	42	35	—	23	405	
	3*	443	17	—	30	52	—	43	43	628	(1469)

Quarterly mean = 366.1
Yearly mean = 1428

*July 1988 only

Source: Information Service for Latin America.

(Pol = Politics; Eco = Economy; Dis = Disaster; Dru = Drug Trafficking; Cor = Corruption; Imm = Immigration; Vio = Violence; Oth = Other)

The *Post* also followed the general pattern, with a more marked surge in reportage in 1985 than the *Times* (table 3). Its reaction to the drug-related murders was much more pronounced, with coverage leaping from virtually nothing to 188 column inches in the first quarter of 1985. The *Post* nearly matched the *Times* coverage of the earthquakes and substantially exceeded the *Times* on political events in the third and fourth quarters of that year. Though the *Times* coverage of economic affairs was more than triple that of the *Post* in the first quarter of 1986, it was surpassed by the Washington daily in the next two quarters. The *Post's* attention returned to drug problems in the first half of 1988 after relative neglect in 1987, and then elections came to the fore in July.

The networks provided generally less consistent coverage of Mexico than the papers, with periods of neglect followed by spurts of interest. Television stresses stories that contain action and vivid imagery—such as gun battles, natural disasters, and violent demonstrations—or dramatic human interest stories, such as hostage situations and rescue operations. This helps explain the extraordinary emphasis placed on the Camarena and earthquake stories in 1985. Arguably, the stories of that year led the networks to stress the Helms hearings even more in 1986. With some minor variations such as NBC's greater attention to immigration, the striking finding is the overall similarity in coverage by the three networks (tables 4, 5, and 6).[13]

---

[13]*Television News Index and Abstracts* is a monthly survey of evening network news that provides the time given to each story along with a brief summary of content.

Table 3. *Washington Post* Coverage of Mexico, 1979-1988 (by calendar quarter, in column inches)

		Pol	Eco	Dis	Dru	Cor	Imm	Vio	Oth	Total	
1979	1	222	212	—	3	—	114	—	63	614	
	2	21	80	—	—	—	32	—	—	133	
	3	143	166	—	—	41	116	—	16	482	
	4	103	42	25	—	—	55	14	25	264	(1493)
1980	1	8	36	—	—	21	18	—	26	109	
	2	11	33	2	—	—	17	2	—	65	
	3	34	21	25	—	—	—	—	—	80	
	4	29	7	—	—	—	3	22	—	61	(315)
1981	1	162	44	—	—	—	25	—	—	231	
	2	23	6	—	—	—	32	28	151	240	
	3	31	46	1	—	34	14	—	21	147	
	4	119	—	—	—	—	—	—	—	119	(737)
1982	1	55	29	2	—	13	—	—	—	99	
	2	17	—	—	—	25	—	—	—	42	
	3	75	175	—	—	15	17	—	—	282	
	4	26	65	—	—	—	—	—	—	91	(514)
1983	1	38	89	1	—	—	—	—	—	128	
	2	79	48	—	—	—	—	—	—	127	
	3	69	73	—	—	56	—	—	—	198	
	4	3	46	—	—	—	32	—	—	84	(537)
1984	1	23	30	—	—	—	13	—	6	72	
	2	21	20	—	22	82	57	13	—	215	
	3	32	69	34	—	—	52	17	—	204	
	4	33	27	60	—	—	—	29	—	149	(640)
1985	1	58	23	1	188	—	8	—	54	332	
	2	55	27	—	126	34	—	14	55	311	
	3	103	68	158	12	—	—	7	28	376	
	4	174	65	22	—	—	10	—	13	384	(1303)
1986	1	4	91	—	71	11	—	—	3	180	
	2	272	317	—	99	37	50	23	65	863	
	3	169	163	14	143	—	—	—	43	532	
	4	2	164	—	—	45	30	—	24	255	(1830)
1987	1	—	65	—	—	70	131	—	39	305	
	2	28	37	—	—	—	17	23	12	117	
	3	54	157	—	31	46	—	—	—	288	
	4	95	27	—	8	—	11	—	—	141	(851)
1988	1	—	35	—	44	—	—	—	—	79	
	2	82	23	—	53	—	—	29	—	187	
	3*	402	23	—	32	24	—	31	—	512	(878)

Quarterly mean = 233.3
Yearly mean = 910

*July 1988 only

Source: Information Service for Latin America.

(Pol = Politics; Eco = Economy; Dis = Disaster; Dru = Drug Trafficking;
Cor = Corruption; Imm = Immigration; Vio = Violence; Oth = Other)

Table 4. ABC News Coverage of Mexico, 1979-1988 (by calendar quarter, in seconds of evening network news)

		Pol	Eco	Dis	Dru	Cor	Imm	Vio	Oth	Total	
1979	1	800	20	20	—	—	—	—	860	1700	
	2	110	120	—	—	—	—	—	—	230	
	3	120	50	750	20	—	—	—	—	940	
	4	75	220	410	—	—	—	—	—	705	(3575)
1980	1	—	—	—	—	—	—	—	—	—	
	2	—	10	20	—	—	110	—	—	140	
	3	—	—	140	—	—	—	—	—	140	
	4	160	—	20	—	—	—	—	—	180	(360)
1981	1	550	—	—	—	—	—	20	200	790	
	2	320	—	—	—	—	—	—	—	320	
	3	50	60	—	—	—	320	—	50	480	
	4	—	—	—	—	—	—	—	—	—	(1590)
1982	1	640	—	—	—	—	—	—	—	640	
	2	—	—	110	—	190	—	—	—	300	
	3	270	660	30	—	—	180	—	20	1160	
	4	70	20	—	—	—	140	—	—	330	(2430)
1983	1	—	280	50	—	—	120	—	—	450	
	2	20	—	—	—	—	—	—	30	50	
	3	780	—	—	—	—	—	—	—	780	
	4	—	190	—	—	—	—	—	—	190	(1470)
1984	1	—	50	—	—	—	—	—	—	50	
	2	240	—	—	—	—	—	—	460	700	
	3	100	—	—	—	—	—	—	240	340	
	4	—	—	220	110	—	—	50	—	380	(1470)
1985	1	580	—	—	1420	—	—	40	—	2040	
	2	—	—	—	230	—	—	60	—	290	
	3	290	—	2250	140	—	—	—	—	2680	
	4	—	—	390	—	—	—	—	120	510	(5520)
1986	1	40	50	140	40	—	—	—	—	270	
	2	240	600	360	440	—	—	—	—	1640	
	3	140	—	—	1060	—	—	—	—	1200	
	4	—	—	—	230	280	—	—	—	510	(3620)
1987	1	—	—	—	—	—	—	—	90	90	
	2	—	—	—	150	—	—	—	80	230	
	3	—	60	10	—	—	170	—	150	390	
	4	20	260	10	—	30	—	—	330	550	(1260)
1988	1	250	—	40	30	—	—	—	160	480	
	2	—	—	10	10	—	250	70	—	320	
	*3	410	—	—	—	—	—	—	—	410	

Quarterly mean = 577.1
Yearly mean = 2251

*July 1988 only

Source: *Television News Index and Abstracts*, various issues.

(Pol = Politics; Eco = Economy; Dis = Disaster; Dru = Drug Trafficking; Cor = Corruption; Imm = Immigration; Vio = Violence; Oth = Other)

Table 5. CBS News Coverage of Mexico, 1979-1988 (by calendar quarter, in seconds of evening network news)

		Pol	Eco	Dis	Dru	Cor	Imm	Vio	Oth	Total	
1979	1	640	410	75	—	—	—	—	740	1865	
	2	230	230	—	—	—	20	—	—	480	
	3	200	130	—	—	—	—	20	—	350	
	4	100	50	210	—	—	—	—	—	360	(3055)
1980	1	60	20	70	—	—	—	—	—	150	
	2	20	20	110	—	—	—	—	—	150	
	3	5	—	50	—	—	—	—	—	55	
	4	200	30	30	—	—	—	—	—	260	(615)
1981	1	430	20	—	—	—	—	—	60	510	
	2	250	190	—	—	—	120	—	—	560	
	3	360	60	140	—	—	290	—	170	1020	
	4	170	—	—	—	—	—	—	—	170	(2260)
1982	1	910	140	60	—	—	—	—	30	1140	
	2	—	—	280	—	—	—	—	—	280	
	3	400	940	190	—	—	180	130	20	1860	
	4	30	80	30	—	—	—	—	—	140	(3470)
1983	1	40	660	—	—	—	180	—	—	880	
	2	20	—	—	—	—	90	—	40	150	
	3	350	170	—	—	—	140	—	—	660	
	4	40	640	—	—	—	—	—	—	680	(2370)
1984	1	—	110	—	—	—	300	—	190	600	
	2	370	—	220	—	—	—	—	—	590	
	3	70	—	—	—	—	—	—	120	190	
	4	—	—	640	140	—	—	140	—	920	(2300)
1985	1	160	90	—	1590	—	—	—	60	1900	
	2	20	—	—	270	—	250	70	—	610	
	3	350	—	2260	130	—	—	—	70	2810	
	4	—	30	300	40	—	—	170	170	710	(6030)
1986	1	20	—	300	260	—	—	—	—	580	
	2	30	430	150	690	—	—	20	210	1530	
	3	500	430	—	780	—	780	—	—		
	4	120	—	—	120	—	60	—	—	300	(4900)
1987	1	—	—	—	110	—	—	—	20	130	
	2	—	—	40	—	—	170	—	—	210	
	3	—	—	120	20	—	360	—	—	500	
	4	—	120	10	70	—	—	—	—	200	(1040)
1988	1	130	—	20	110	—	—	—	—	260	
	2	30	—	30	10	—	180	120	160	530	
	3*	760	—	80	—	—	—	—	—	840	

Quarterly mean = 709.5
Yearly mean = 2767

* July 1988 only

Source: *Television News Index and Abstracts*, various issues.

(Pol = Politics; Eco = Economy; Dis = Disaster; Dru = Drug Trafficking;
Cor = Corruption; Imm = Immigration; Vio = Violence; Oth = Other)

Table 6. NBC News Coverage of Mexico, 1979-1988 (by calendar quarters, in seconds of evening network news)

		Pol	Eco	Dis	Dru	Cor	Imm	Vio	Oth	Total	
1979	1	500	300	50	—	—	—	—	1100	1950	
	2	100	—	80	—	—	—	—	—	180	
	3	30	110	—	—	—	—	—	—	140	
	4	290	120	340	—	—	—	—	—	750	(3020)
1980	1	50	—	—	—	—	500	—	—	550	
	2	—	10	70	—	—	110	—	—	190	
	3	30	—	80	—	—	—	—	—	110	
	4	380	—	—	—	—	180	—	—	560	(1410)
1981	1	510	—	—	—	—	—	—	—	510	
	2	700	—	—	—	—	—	—	220	920	
	3	350	100	20	—	—	390	—	130	990	
	4	120	—	—	—	—	—	—	30	150	(2570)
1982	1	1230	50	—	—	—	—	—	210	1300	
	2	—	—	160	—	—	—	—	—	160	
	3	260	450	30	90	110	110	—	—	1050	
	4	70	250	—	—	20	—	—	60	400	(2910)
1983	1	10	180	290	—	—	170	—	10	660	
	2	60	—	160	—	—	—	—	—	220	
	3	170	150	110	—	—	20	—	—	450	
	4	20	-50	—	—	—	—	—	—	70	(1400)
1984	1	150	100	—	—	—	—	—	—	250	
	2	80	60	—	—	—	220	—	—	360	
	3	—	130	—	60	—	—	—	810	1000	
	4	30	—	560	—	—	270	20	—	880	(2490)
1985	1	130	—	—	1260	—	—	—	—	1390	
	2	60	—	—	250	—	—	130	—	440	
	3	300	40	3060	90	—	—	—	—	3490	
	4	—	110	780	—	—	—	—	130	1020	(6340)
1986	1	40	200	180	260	—	—	—	—	680	
	2	40	520	320	580	—	270	—	40	1770	
	3	300	—	—	680	—	250	—	200	1430	
	4	30	—	30	40	—	—	—	—	100	(3980)
1987	1	—	220	—	—	—	—	—	160	380	
	2	—	170	—	—	—	—	—	—	170	
	3	—	—	150	—	—	420	—	150	720	
	4	—	120	30	—	—	—	—	—	150	(1420)
1988	1	—	280	200	260	—	—	—	160	900	
	2	—	—	50	—	—	140	120	160	370	
	3*	310	—	—	—	—	—	—	—	310	

Quarterly mean = 695.4
Yearly mean = 2712

* July 1988 only

Source: *Television News Index and Abstracts*, various issues.

(Pol = Politics; Eco = Economy; Dis = Disaster; Dru = Drug Trafficking; Cor = Corruption; Imm = Immigration; Vio = Violence; Oth = Other)

The importance of the Camarena story of February–March 1985 must be underlined. The *Post* covered the story extensively, but the networks reacted with surprising emphasis. Television had largely ignored the drug issue between 1979 and 1984, especially with respect to Mexico. Then in 1985 the three networks devoted 92.5 minutes, including seven lead stories, to Camarena alone. In addition, I calculated another 17.5 minutes of drug-related stories closely tied to Camarena[14] that led me to search for an explanation for the intensity of this coverage.

The Camarena incident combined elements of both medium and moment. First, television stresses the visually dramatic, such as this story of a U.S. agent killed on the front lines of the battle against drug trafficking. Second, attention to drug abuse as an issue was rapidly accelerating throughout U.S. society, a concern reflected in attention by both politicians and the media: President Reagan's wife, for example, had previously launched a drug awareness campaign. Third, for a variety of reasons largely relating to frustration about lack of cooperation, U.S. officials were more willing than before to voice their impatience with what they regarded as insufficient cooperation by Mexican authorities. This added political dimension reinforced the coverage. In all, it was as though the United States, unable to resolve its drug abuse problems, vented its frustration on that specific incident.

Whatever the reasons, the timing and intensity of the Camarena incident served to color subsequent reporting. Network news, which heretofore had only perfunctorily announced the results of Mexico's presidential elections, had previously ignored the midterm affairs entirely. This time, considerable attention (15.7 minutes) was brought to bear on alleged official fraud, especially in Sonora and Nuevo León. The earthquakes, though reported as major disaster stories, probably further damaged the overall image of the Mexican government. The generally negative cast carried over into the Helms hearings and related stories in 1986, such as allegations of electoral fraud in Chihuahua. Then the Cortez incident reignited the fires.

Coinciding with the presidential summit in August, the abduction and mistreatment of DEA agent Victor Cortez by state police in Guadalajara magnified television coverage. President Reagan had drawn attention to the problem of drug trafficking and sought

---

[14]That is, reports on the Camarena incident sandwiched between other stories on drug problems or linked to stories on border searches, corruption, and so forth.

to enlist Mexican cooperation in stepping up programs of inter-
diction. Beginning on 10 August and running to the end of that
month, network news devoted nearly forty-three minutes, including four lead stories, to the problem of drugs and Mexico. As might
be expected, coverage did not focus just on drugs but ranged over
a series of by-now familiar concerns such as corruption, authoritarianism, public insecurity, and lack of cooperation with U.S.
authorities.[15]

In retrospect, 1986 was a particularly difficult year. The following year saw a considerable decline in television coverage, but—
like the print media—attention focused sharply on the 1988 presidential elections.

Although these data report quantities of news coverage, a word
on quality is in order before discussing implications for the bilateral relation. The sparse literature on media coverage of Mexico
has stressed weaknesses rather than bias.

> We can conclude from this study—and we are
> certain other such studies would bear us out—that
> American newspaper readers have a very incom-
> plete, shallow, gap-filled and fuzzy image of their
> neighbors to the south. Certainly, if such important
> and cosmopolitan dailies as the *New York Times, Los
> Angeles Times,* and *Washington Post* give so little
> attention to Mexico, we can assume that smaller
> newspapers in the U.S. do an even poorer job of
> reporting and interpreting the activities of Mexico.[16]

Another commentator contrasted U.S. press coverage of Mexico
unfavorably with reporting by Canadians and Europeans.

> [U.S.] journalists have often seemed to see Mexico
> in much the same fashion as tourists at a border-
> town market, coming back with a kind of curio

---

[15]For example, the summary of ABC news of 18 August reports: "Death of DEA
secretary in Guadalajara, Susan Hoefler in traffic accident reported.... Last year's
torture-murder in Guadalajara of DEA agent Enrique Camarena recalled; DEA said
considering pulling agents from area. Withdrawal of U.S. agents from Mazatlán
noted due to threats from drug trafficker Manuel 'Crazy Pig' Salsito; details given."
[16]John C. Merrill and Whitney R. Mundt, "U.S. Daily Newspaper Coverage of
Mexico," study conducted for the USICA, Washington, D.C., and presented in
Washington at Journalists' Symposium, 17-20 May, 1981, p. 31. The authors surveyed two separate weeks, relatively slack periods, in late December 1980 and early
January 1981 (see tables 3 and 4).

coverage ... [I]t rarely captures the reality beneath the surface. While the crisis has produced some attentive reporting (and more than twenty full-time Mexico City correspondents representing twenty-seven U.S. news organizations), the shallow, belated, and rather helter-skelter nature of Mexican coverage as a whole seems woefully inadequate for a story that is taking place so close at hand.[17]

Television does no better. A study of television reporting on the 1982 economic crisis and 1985 earthquake "found not much subconscious bias in the selection of stories or priority of facts within a given story," but rather "a tendency of U.S. television journalists to report the public life of Mexico rarely, and fragmentedly."[18]

In short, while the media have done much to raise Mexico's standing in the U.S. issue agenda, they have done less to inform the public. Even so, the coverage of the 1988 elections showed improvement. Among the reasons for this, it appears that learning took place on the parts of both U.S. journalists and Mexican political actors. Important as well was the apparent perception by the media that significant changes were unfolding in Mexican politics.

IMPLICATIONS FOR THE BILATERAL RELATION

To this point I have shown that media attention to Mexico peaked in 1979, rose somewhat in 1982, and made a marked resurgence in 1985-1986, with the possibility of another upsurge in 1988. I asserted, but did not demonstrate, that much of the 1985-86 coverage was negative, unbalanced, and superficial. In this section I take the further risk of speculating on the linkages between media coverage and the bilateral relationship, commenting first on recent tendencies in mass and elite opinion and then on an issue of some significance for Mexican internal politics in 1985: the phenomenon of so-called *neopanismo* and the midterm elections.

---

[17]Roger Morris, "Mexico: The U.S. Press Takes a Siesta," *Columbia Journalism Review* (January-February 1985), p. 31.
[18]Marvin Alisky, "U.S. Television Network Portrayal of Mexican Crises," paper presented at the annual conference of the International Studies Association-Southwest, San Antonio, Texas, 21 March, 1986, p. 12.

With respect to mass opinion in the United States, a Harris survey taken in July 1986 found that

> Basically, the public in this country has strong sympathies for the people just south of the border and the problems they face. Above all else, Mexico is seen in friendly, positive terms by the American people. But the public here is also deeply worried and distressed by the full platter of troubles that are plaguing that country.[19]

By a large (75-18 percent) majority, most of the respondents expressed a genuine affinity for Mexico. But they also indicated concern over illegal drugs, the debt, official corruption, electoral fraud, and illegal migration. Interesting contradictions appeared with respect to bilateral relations: the survey showed significant deterioration of public confidence in Mexico as an ally (see table 7), but at the same time, respondents expressed confidence that differences between the two countries with regard to Nicaragua could be settled. Furthermore, by a 59-29 margin, respondents thought the Helms' hearings hurt bilateral relations.[20]

It would appear that despite the upsurge of unfavorable media coverage, public opinion about Mexico in the United States showed relatively little deterioration, except with regard to Mexico as an ally. Even here, however, Mexico's policy toward Nicaragua is one of the few problem areas where respondents believed improvements were possible.

Table 7. U.S. Opinion about Mexico as an Ally, July 1986

	1986 percent	1984 percent
Close ally	20	34
Friendly but not an ally	55	56
Not friendly but not an enemy	17	6
Unfriendly and an enemy	1	1
Not sure	7	3

Question: "In general, do you feel that Mexico is a close ally of the United States, friendly but not a close ally, not friendly but not an enemy, or is unfriendly and an enemy of the U.S.?"

Source: *Harris Survey*, 1986, no. 44, p. 3.

---

[19]*Harris Survey*, 1986, no. 44, p. 1.
[20]*Harris Survey*, 1986, no. 44, p. 4.

Time series data from Gallup for the 1976-87 period paint a more troubling picture. Table 8 shows that those indicating a favorable impression of Mexico comprise a fairly steady share in the mid-50 percent range; however, those expressing a very favorable opinion dropped from 20 to 11 percent of the sample, and those expressing an unfavorable opinion increased from 14 to 23 percent.

Table 8. Trend for Scalometer Rating of Mexico, 1976-1987

	April/May 1987 percent	February 1979 percent	June 1976 percent
Very Favorable (+4, +5)	11	21	20
Favorable (+1, +2, +3)	56	51	55
Unfavorable (-1, -2, -3)	23	16	14
Very Unfavorable (-4, -5)	4	5	3
Dont' Know	6	7	8
Sample Size	(2169)	(1534)	(1544)
Source:	Times Mirror/ Gallup	Gallup Poll	Gallup Poll

Question: (Hand respondent card X) "Notice that the boxes on this card go from the highest position of +5 for a country you have a very favorable opinion of all the way down to the lowest position of a -5 for a country that you have a very unfavorable opinion of. How far up the scale or how far down the scale would you rate ... (read list of countries)."

With only limited survey data at hand, elite opinion in the United States is more difficult to characterize. The demographic breakdown of the 1987 Gallup/Times Mirror data shows little significant variation in attitudes toward Mexico among categories of respondents. As exceptions, Jews express more unfavorable attitudes than the sample average (40-23 percent), as do college graduates under 30 years of age (31-23 percent). Overall, college graduates express both slightly more favorable (70-67 percent) as well as less favorable (25-27 percent) views than the average. These findings are repeated for those scoring highest in knowledge about foreign countries.[21]

With respect to possible linkages between attitudes and types of media, it appears to make little difference whether respondents relied principally on print or television, although those who claimed to watch network news regularly indicated less favorable

---

[21]This is due to a smaller "No opinion" response.

views toward Mexico than those who said they hardly ever watch network news (29-21 percent).[22]

On a strictly personal note, as one who has attended more than a few meetings on Mexico over the past decade, my impression is that nonspecialists reached by different routes and at different paces the general conclusions that Mexican stability could no longer be taken for granted, that Mexico confronts profound structural problems, and that there are no obvious solutions. The frequent prescription, not surprisingly, was to recommend one or another dose of "Americanism." Typically suggested were less government and greater freedom for market forces, more political democracy, and greater efforts to eliminate corruption. The notion that all good things go together is striking; if Mexico would open the political process (read let the opposition win) the resulting rise in investor and citizen confidence would enhance recovery. A comment after the 1985 elections, for example:

> If a country is so unwilling to accept political change, can it carry out the tough economic reforms necessary to solve the long-running economic crisis? Can the political elite give up some short-term power in favor of long-term stability?[23]

Shifting the focus, without considerable survey evidence I cannot draw causal linkages between U.S. media penetration into Mexico and trends in mass opinion in that country about the United States. Two channels are significant. U.S. media messages are transmitted directly to Mexican elites; they are also sought out and filtered by Mexican media.

U.S. media directly reach growing numbers of Mexicans. Though I have no recent circulation figures for major dailies and news magazines, the *New York Times, Wall Street Journal, Time,* and *Newsweek* are readily available in Mexico City. The news magazines also reach other major cities throughout the country. U.S. commercial television networks are accessible via cable television to 353,680

---

[22]Interestingly, those approving of President Reagan appear slightly more favorable toward Mexico (69-67 percent) than those who disapprove of him (65-67 percent). Ticket-splitters (Republican presidential/Democratic Congress) are significantly more unfavorable toward Mexico (38-27 percent), and "weak liberals" are more negative than the average (32-27 percent), as are "strong conservatives" (33-27 percent).

[23]Steve Frazier, *Wall Street Journal,* 12 July 1985.

Mexican homes as of 1987, supplemented by an estimated 100,000 satellite dishes, largely in northern Mexico.[24] One firm, Cablevisión, S.A., claims to serve a half million people in Mexico City with news from the major networks as well as the Cable News Network. The Mexican government's concern over direct news broadcasting by U.S. media is seen in occasional censorship of cable television.

> Interference with U.S. news programs was especially frequent earlier this year [1985] when Mexico's narcotics trade was under scrutiny, acknowledged Mexican officials, who said they have the legal obligation to block local broadcasting of what they view as hostile or distorted news coverage.[25]

Apart from direct consumption of U.S. media through print and electronic channels, stories are reported through the Mexican media. Mexican newspapers have long relied heavily on U.S.-based wire services and prestige papers for news concerning the United States and international events. Thus, messages selected and filtered for a U.S. audience are routinely collected and refiltered to Mexican readers. Also, Mexican media have operated with relatively greater freedom from government censorship since the early 1970s. There is a richer variety of commentary, much of it critical of government actions. By extension, positive as well as negative foreign stories receive greater circulation than before.

Again without claiming a causal link between media and attitudes, table 9 reports trends in general opinion of the United States by Mexico City residents during 1956-85. The findings suggest that favorable attitudes toward the United States held up remarkably well in the midst of economic crisis after 1981, albeit with some variation, and that with the exception of 1984-85 attitudes among the general population have been generally more favorable than among the "better educated."

Despite the overall favorable opinion about the United States, the majority of the better educated respondents held that this country treats Mexico unfairly in matters of mutual concern. University graduates were the most critical (65 percent to 34

---

[24]M. Delal Baer, "The Press," in *Prospects for Mexico*, ed. George Grayson (Washington, D.C.: Foreign Service Institute, 1988), p. 108.
[25]William Orme, Jr., *Washington Post*, 13 July 1985.

Table 9. Trends in General Opinion of the U.S.: Net Favorable Opinion Scores in Mexico City, 1956-1985

	Jan. 1956	Mar. 1972	Jan. 1979	Aug. 1979	Dec. 1980	Mar. 1981	July 1983	Nov. 1983	Oct.-Jan. 1984-85
For better educated	—	—	+41	+51	+46	—	+32	+50	+69
For general population	+57	+39	+48	+55	—	+51	+45	—	+65*

* Separate survey in same time frame by a different firm.

Source: Adapted from table 2 of William J. Millard, "Better-Educated Mexican Opinion on Key Political and Economic Issues," R-22-85 (Washington, D.C.: Office of Research, United States Information Agency, September 1985), p.16.

percent). Regionally, Mexico City respondents were more negative in their assessment of U.S. fairness (60 percent versus 40 percent), whereas the cities to the north were actually favorable to the U.S., a majority of the better-educated publics in Monterrey (57 percent), Juarez (54 percent), and Tijuana (57 percent) saying Mexico is treated equitably. The same was true in Veracruz (58 percent).[26] Nevertheless, 65 percent of the better-educated named the United States as the country Mexico should work with most closely to benefit its own economic interests.[27]

These data were gathered before the burst of U.S. media attention to Mexico in 1985 and 1986. A *New York Times* survey, taken in October-November 1986, may indicate some deterioration of favorable attitudes held by the Mexican public about the government and people of the United States (see table 10). Nevertheless,

Table 10. Mexican Public Opinion about the Government and People of the United States, November 1986 (national sample, in percentages)

	Attitude toward U.S. government	Attitude toward U.S. people
Favorable	48	47
Unfavorable	27	22
Don't know	25	30

Questions: "In general, would you say that your opinion of the United States government (people of the United States) is favorable, unfavorable, or don't you know enough about it to have an opinion?"

Source: *New York Times* Poll, "Mexico Survey, October 28-November 4, 1986," mimeo, p. 6.

---

[26]William J. Millard, "Better-Educated Mexican Opinion on Key Political and Economic Issues," R-22-85 (Washington, D.C.: Office of Research, United States Information Agency, September 1985), p. 12.
[27]William J. Millard, "Better-Educated Mexican Opinion," p. 9

by a 66-33 percent margin, respondents described relations between Mexico and the United States as "friendly" or "very friendly."

Since the 1960s Mexican elites have acquired an increased awareness, gained through travel and study abroad, of foreign opinion about Mexico. Thus, the urban middle sectors are more sensitive to foreign commentary at the same time that the internal crisis deepens. Further, the rise of the technical elite, along with the relative displacement of the politicians, serves as a mechanism to amplify external comment throughout government.[28]

U.S. media affect Mexican internal politics more directly than just through public opinion. As noted previously, since the early 1970s Mexican politics grew more conflictive as several pacts came under strain in such important and diverse areas as government relations with the intelligentsia, organized labor, business, the middle sectors, the Catholic church, and the United States. These tensions both resulted from and contributed to deterioration of the economy. In short, Mexico is squarely in the midst of its worst crisis since at least 1929.

President Miguel de la Madrid (1982-88) was publicly committed to promoting significant changes in the Mexican economy and polity but on terms acceptable to the regime. This implied economic modernization with opening toward the regional and global systems, but with the survival of a strong presidential system based on the dominant Institutional Revolutionary party (PRI) and government bureaucracy. The equation in terms of the "high politics" of bilateral relations was that good relations with the United States are more important than ever (with respect to trade and investment, for example), but not at the cost of endangering regime survival. In fact, an important element of Mexican statecraft is fine-tuning anti-U.S. sentiment to bolster regime popularity and legitimacy without endangering policies of honoring debt obligations and encouraging foreign investment.[29]

---

[28]See Levy, "The Political Consequence of Changing Socialization Patterns," and Peter H. Smith, "Leadership and Change: Intellectuals and Technocrats in Mexico," in Camp, *Mexico's Political Stability*, pp. 101-118. Norman Bailey and Richard Cohen, in *The Mexican Time Bomb* (New York: Priority Press, 1987), pp. 20-23, suggest that the *técnicos'* sensitivity to foreign opinion about Mexico acts as a deterrent to debt default.
[29]I set out my own understanding of these issues in *Governing Mexico: The Statecraft of Crisis Management* (New York: St. Martin's, 1988).

In the context of transition-with-survival, a number of issues are particularly conflictive internally and neuralgic with respect to foreign—especially U.S.—comment. An ad hoc list of the more important ones might include:

- Nonintervention in Mexican internal affairs
  - The role of the state in society and the economy
  - The status of foreign investment
  - The meaning of democracy and role of elections
  - Legal freedoms and responsibilities
  - Human rights
  - Standards of ethics in government and society

- Autonomy in foreign policy
  - Participation in trade regimes
  - Participation in international organizations
  - Migration
  - Central America

One might demonstrate at length how foreign media comment can inflame any of these issues, but I shall make the point with democracy and the 1985 midterm elections.

Democracy in Mexico connotes not only individual freedoms and contested elections, but also nationalism and the improvement of living conditions of the poor. In a more complete ideological formulation, the PRI as the embodiment of the Revolution is committed to using state power to guarantee national autonomy and improved social welfare for the "majorities."[30] In the period of normalcy, roughly from 1946-70, there was a certain consistency of nationalism, social welfare, and electoral victory. In short, the PRI could usually win elections honestly and easily (though it probably inflated the turnout numbers). With the problems of the 1980s, the PRI-government has had to resort to fraud to a greater—though still limited—extent.[31] This sort of practice is more costly and difficult, however, given enhanced internal press freedom and

---

[30]"Majorities" refers to the organized elements of workers, peasants, and middle-strata citizenry.

[31]As a very rough guess, of the three hundred national congressional electoral districts, in 1985 the PRI faced difficult opposition in about fifty and might conceivably have lost in as many as thirty. The 1986 *New York Times* poll cited in table 10 reported (p. 3) that 42 percent indicated that they had voted for the PRI in the last presidential election. The next highest number (25 percent) had abstained, and 12 percent indicated that they had voted for the principal opposition party, the PAN.

greater external attention to Mexican politics. Especially since 1982, the electoral challenge to the PRI is most acute along the northern border with the United States, an area where higher living standards, impatience with centralism, a stronger private sector, more active opposition, and democratic demonstration effect from the United States all converge.

As the midterm elections of July 1985 approached, the de la Madrid government experienced pressures from several quarters. The austerity program imposed in order to qualify for international lending assistance worsened government relations with society in general and in particular with organized labor, the backbone of the party. Broad sectors of public opinion held the United States responsible in good part for Mexico's economic troubles.[32] The president had extended his "moral renovation" campaign to include honest elections and had promised to respect the vote. Nevertheless, the setbacks suffered by the PRI in the 1983 state and local elections probably led to second thoughts at the higher levels of government and party.

By 1985 the PAN had become a more formidable opponent, especially in the north, and had enlisted the U.S. media in its campaign against the government. The PAN's success in this was boosted in part by the PRI's generally inept style of dealing with foreign media. Further, U.S. Ambassador John Gavin created considerable press stir within Mexico and launched yet another round of harsh commentary between Gavin and the PRI leadership by meeting with PAN leaders in Sonora in 1984.[33] In December 1984 and January 1985 PAN militants became embroiled in violent protests, amply covered by U.S. media, against alleged electoral fraud in the northern border town of Piedras Negras.

The border incidents, economic recession, strong opposition showing in previous elections, and presidential statements all

---

[32]Millard, "Better-Educated Mexican Opinion," p. 10, reports that 46 percent of the respondents stated that U.S. economic policies were harmful to Mexico. "Detailed analysis shows that larger proportions of university graduates than other educated tended to say U.S. policies are harmful."

[33]Many Mexicans I talked with during 1983-85 were convinced that Ambassador Gavin's freewheeling style and outspoken criticisms of Mexican government and press were yet another piece of a U.S. government campaign to put pressure on Mexico. My own impression was that Gavin's temperament and status as a political appointee led him to assume a less orthodox diplomatic role. Whatever the case, Gavin's style certainly complicated the bilateral relation and Mexico's internal politics in 1985.

created great expectations for the July 1985 elections, and the foreign press assembled as never before in anticipation of an interesting story. Either the opposition would win important victories, perhaps even a governorship, or the PRI government would have to resort to fraud—in which case there would be violence.

From the government's perspective, the situation represented a tactical dilemma with important strategic implications. If the government permitted free elections, the opposition might make important gains (though it probably would not win a governorship), which might awaken more general expectations about elections throughout Mexico. This in turn would intensify conflicts within the dominant party and might create uncertainties that could reduce investor confidence. On the other hand, if the government employed obvious fraud then the foreign media would get part of its story; if violence resulted, the press reaction would be only part of a more serious problem of internal order and business confidence.[34]

There is no evidence to support any conclusion, but it is likely that the government had opted to control the elections even before the deluge of media criticism burst forth in February and March 1985. This would seem to be the gist of government and party speeches to the effect that Mexico would practice its own forms of democracy and would not be deceived by artificial foreign examples. Foreign media criticism, to speculate further, probably strengthened the arguments of those within the PRI-government that Mexico could not show weakness on fundamental issues of internal autonomy and that the PAN should not be rewarded for enlisting support from U.S. officials and media. Given the considerable political costs of the austerity program, the leadership probably needed little persuasion to hold the line.

In any event, considerable fraud was detected by foreign reporters in both Sonora and Nuevo León, but there was relatively little violence as a result.[35] The media outcry, internal and foreign, was considerable, and the Mexican government incurred a substantial penalty for its policy.[36] Reporter Sam Dillon put it well:

---

[34]For a more extended analysis see Delal Baer and John Bailey, "Mexico's 1985 Midterm Elections: A Preliminary Assessment," *LASA Forum*, Winter 1985.

[35]Some violence was reported in San Luis Río Colorado, Sonora, and in Monterrey, Nuevo León.

[36]In the Mexican press, see especially the stories in *Proceso* 454 (July 15):10-29; and 455 (July 22):10-13; and also in the Monterrey dailies, *El Porvenir*, July 2, and *El Norte*, July 6-11. In the U.S. press see the stories by Robert Meislin, *New York Times*,

"Virtually no independent observer in Mexico trusts those results, and the immediate cost to the government of asserting them has been paid in the scrip of national credibility."[37]

Following the criticisms of the 1985 election, the Mexican government stepped up its efforts to educate the foreign media and to get across its own version of a true picture of the political situation, as opposed to the distortions alleged by the PAN and other enemies. Yet with the 1986 Chihuahua elections, something like a "Sonora syndrome" had taken hold with the foreign media. The opposition's complaints of electoral fraud in the local and gubernatorial races were widely noted in the U.S. media before the balloting, and the government's subsequent electoral victories were accordingly stigmatized.

Although the Sonora syndrome remained a factor in the coverage of the presidential succession of 1988, other themes became more significant and the overall tone became more positive.[38] The appearance of the Democratic Current, a dissident faction within the PRI, drew more attention to the infighting leading up to the nomination of Carlos Salinas de Gortari in October 1987. In the campaign, Salinas's avowed commitment to modernize Mexico was contrasted with the resurgence of populism with Cuauhtémoc Cárdenas, candidate of the Democratic Front. The PAN's candidate, Manuel Clouthier, was rather lost from view, and the significance of the change taking place overshadowed, but did not eliminate, themes of electoral fraud. When reports of the electoral results were delayed, most reporters simply recorded the statements of government and opposition spokesmen. And when the results were announced, reporters conveyed the opposition's protests less emphatically than in 1985. The press concentrated nearly as much on the struggle within the PRI as on the significance of the elections, and editorial comments were generally more positive about the elections, noting that Mexico had begun the transition toward genuine democracy.[39]

July 9, 16; Steve Frazier, *Wall Street Journal*, July 12; William Orme, *Washington Post*, July 8; Dennis Volman, *Christian Science Monitor*, July 9; and Bruno Lopez, *Arizona Republic*, July 28. Robert McCartney, *Washington Post*, July 11, p. A24, put it most bluntly: "Several reporters said that less respect was shown for laws and procedures in Sonora than in the elections they covered in El Salvador and Nicaragua."
[37]*Miami Herald*, July 12, 1985. A problem with the U.S. press was the apparent callousness of the local PRI. For example, Dillon reports a PRI official in Sonora commenting to a reporter, "this is not going to be a little dog biting the policeman. This is going to be the policeman kicking the little dog."
[38]My comment on this period draws on research by Leopoldo Gómez.
[39]For example, see the *Wall Street Journal*, July 11, 1988, p. 18.

CONCLUSIONS

This study is consistent with recent assessments of the current state of U.S.-Mexican relations, which tend to stress the increased problems and difficulties. The broader structural changes in the regional and global systems suggest greater strains and adjustments for both countries, quite apart from the bilateral relation. At the same time, the countries are becoming more closely interrelated in a variety of ways. Rather than promoting greater harmony, this heightened integration will likely generate more points of contention.

The typical recommendation, a bromide usually, is to promote greater mutual understanding at both popular and elite levels. This discussion of media suggests a particular focus in mutual understanding. Obviously, it is especially important to examine the core societal values that shape the ways in which news is created and interpreted. Democracy, for example, means different things to various groups in the two societies. It is as problematic for U.S. commentators to equate democracy with electoral competition as it is for Mexicans to discount the profound importance of free elections to both elite and popular beliefs in the United States.

More specifically, a better understanding of the operations of the media is required. Since this chapter dealt with the U.S. media, the recommendation that flows from the discussion is that Mexican elites require a clearer understanding of the complex and dynamic webs that connect the U.S. media with social and political actors and with public opinion more broadly considered. At a minimum, closer study will show that the U.S. media suffer attack from many groups, including the government, virtually all of the time.

The 1988 elections opened a new phase in the media dimension of the bilateral relation, with aspects that suggest both conflict and comity. Most importantly, Mexican reality changed. Despite the many allegations of fraud, the U.S. media focused on a fundamental transformation in Mexican politics: the old PRI system was finished; something new was emerging. The perception of real change contributed to more balanced coverage.

At the same time that the 1988 elections brought a brief improvement in the tone of U.S. media coverage, they unleashed forces that could contribute to heightened tensions in the bilateral relation. The elections underlined the resurgence of a potent form of Mexican populism. Cárdenas, the Democratic Front candidate, ran on a platform of nationalism, economic growth, debt relief, benefits to the poor, and honest elections. Given the tensions that have accumulated on these issues over the past six years, powerful forces found expression in the electoral process. Depending on the outcome of many economic and political factors, especially debt relief and growth, these forces may complicate the bilateral relation.

When the U.S. media began to pay attention to Mexico after 1979, an important theme was their criticism of authoritarian practices, especially with respect to elections. In 1988 the media applauded the apparent democratic opening. It now remains to be seen how these same media will perceive and interpret the pent-up demands and frustrations that have been released as part of that opening.

SECTION

II

SOURCES

4

To View a Neighbor: The Hollywood Textbook on Mexico

Carlos E. Cortés

In 1836, faced with the independence uprising of the northeastern corner of Mexico known as Texas, a Mexican army force led by General Antonio López de Santa Anna captured the San Antonio mission, the Alamo. In the process he defeated Texas troops led by Colonel William Travis and including Davy Crockett and William Bowie. In 1960, Santa Anna captured the Alamo again, this time defeating Texas troops led by John Wayne and including Richard Widmark, Laurence Harvey, and Frankie Avalon. Since then the Alamo has been captured again and again and again by Mexican army commanders ranging from Peter Ustinov to Raúl Julia.

The first event occurred in reality. The succeeding repetitions of the mission were captured on film in such movies as *The Alamo* (1960) and *Viva Max!* (1969), as well as in the 1986 television docudrama, *The Alamo: 13 Days to Glory*. For the American viewing

I would like to thank the Ford Foundation for a grant that helped support my research; Carlos Monsiváis and James Sandos for their insightful comments on a preliminary version of this article; and my research assistant, Thomas Thompson, for his tireless and perceptive collaboration in developing our Ethnicity and Foreignness in Film Computer Data Bank, from which much of the evidence for this article is drawn. My book-in-progress on the U.S. feature film treatment of foreign nations places the depiction of Mexico in the comparative context of Hollywood's changing portrayal of the world, while my book on the movie treatment of ethnic groups will examine Mexican-Americans comparatively with other U.S. ethnic groups.

public, these media creations have provided chapters in Hollywood's long-running, still-unfolding, and often-disturbing American visual media textbook on Mexico.

Has this media textbook fostered better American understanding of Mexico or contributed to a distorted vision of the United States' neighbor to the south? To gain insight into this question we need to analyze the development of the media curriculum through a careful examination of the history of U.S. visual media treatment of Mexico.[1] First, however, we need to address an even more basic question—do fictional movies and television really teach? Or, turning the question around, do viewers learn from the fictional media? The answer, quite simply, is yes, although we need to use restraint in concluding what viewers have learned, just as teachers need to use restraint about concluding what students have learned from their lectures and assigned readings.

While teaching and learning are not synonymous, decades of communications research have demonstrated that feature films and fictional television (including but not limited to docudramas) have had a substantial impact on public perceptions of different world areas, nations, and even component groups within a society such as ethnic groups and women. For example, in a pioneering study in the 1930s, Ruth C. Peterson and L.L. Thurstone showed that viewing the classic silent film *The Birth of a Nation* (1915), which included derogatory depictions of blacks, increased student prejudice toward black Americans.[2] Irwin C. Rosen found that showing the anti-anti-Semitism film *Gentleman's Agreement* (1947) improved student attitudes toward Jews even though most of the tested students stated that the film had not changed their attitudes.[3]

---

[1]Mexican film historian Emilio García Riera has identified over three thousand international films that deal with Mexico or Mexicans, most of them having been made in the United States. His book *México visto por el cine extranjero, 1894-1940* (Guadalajara: Centro de Investigaciones y Enseñanzas Cinematográficas, Universidad de Guadalajara, 1987) includes the most encyclopedic examination yet published on the evolution of the treatment of Mexico in U.S. films up to World War II. Early Mexican-content films are summarized in the 39-page appendix of George H. Roeder, Jr.'s "Mexicans in the Movies: The Image of Mexicans in American Films, 1894-1947" (unpublished manuscript, University of Wisconsin, Madison, 1971), cited in Arthur G. Pettit, *Images of the Mexican American in Fiction and Film* (edited with an afterword by Dennis E. Showalter) (College Station: Texas A&M University Press, 1980), p. 132.

[2]Ruth C. Peterson and L.L. Thurstone, *Motion Pictures and the Social Attitudes of Children* (New York: Macmillan, 1933), pp. 35-38.

[3]Irwin C. Rosen, "The Effect of the Motion Picture 'Gentleman's Agreement' on Attitudes toward Jews," *Journal of Psychology* 26 (1948):525-536.

More recently, psychologist Bradley S. Greenberg reported that 40 percent of the white children he was studying believed that television shows accurately portrayed blacks, even though these shows contrasted with their own personal experiences with blacks.[4]

The teaching power of the entertainment media has not escaped the notice of societal groups and even governments. The National Association for the Advancement of Colored People led a protest movement against *The Birth of a Nation*, recognizing its impact on the image of blacks. In 1938 Poland banned the film *Show Boat* (1936) on the grounds that its classic song, "Ol' Man River," was "proletarian propaganda."[5] And media concerns have surfaced continually in Washington. In 1941, responding angrily to what he viewed as a Hollywood campaign to propel the United States into World War II, isolationist Senator Gerald Nye of North Dakota exclaimed: "But when you go to the movies, you go there to be entertained .... And then the picture starts—goes to work on you .... Before you know where you are you have actually listened to a speech designed to make you believe that Hitler is going to get you if you don't watch out."[6]

In recent years, ethnic groups have protested strongly against media depictions of themselves as criminal and violent. Reacting to such pressures and reluctantly admitting the negative teaching potential of their fictional products, television producers and filmmakers have resorted to various stratagems. For example, they have grafted ineffectual disclaimers onto such films as *The Godfather* (Italian-Americans), *Year of the Dragon* (Chinese-Americans), and *Scarface* (Cuban-Americans), claiming that these movies are not meant to represent any specific ethnic group.

Clearly, visual media do teach whether or not media-makers created them with any pedagogical intention.[7] Visual media have the potential for influencing any viewer. For people who have never visited or read substantially about another country, films and

---

[4]Bradley S. Greenberg, "Children's Reactions to TV Blacks," *Journalism Quarterly* 49 (Spring 1972):5-14.

[5]Leo C. Rosten, *Hollywood: The Movie Colony* (New York: Harcourt, Brace, 1941), p. 356.

[6]Gerald P. Nye, "Our Madness Increases as Our Emergency Shrinks," *Vital Speeches* 7 (15 September 1941), p. 722.

[7]A recent examination of the impact of the visual media on public opinion can be found in Wayne Harold Ault, "Show Business and Politics: The Influence of Television, Entertainment Celebrities, and Motion Pictures on American Public Opinion and Political Behavior" (Ph.D. dissertation, Saint Louis University, 1981).

television may be their main source of information about it.[8] For
example, for tens of millions of Americans, particularly the majority who have neither lived in nor studied about Mexico, motion
pictures and television may be the primary contributors to their
images of Mexico and Mexicans. Moreover, casual moviegoers or
television watchers do not concern themselves with the challenge
of critical thinking or the categorical issues of content analysis. They
usually want to be entertained, distracted, absorbed, stimulated,
or diverted.[9] It is the rare viewer indeed who consciously attempts
to keep Mexico intellectually separate from the rest of Latin America, and Mexicans separate from Mexican-Americans in feature
films. When it comes to Mexico, then, viewer learning may result
not only from the depictions of Mexicans and Mexico, but also of
Mexican-Americans and Latin America in general.

This brings us back to the original question, what have
American motion pictures taught about Mexico? The following conclusions are based on the long-term research for a two-volume
work-in-progress on the history of U.S. feature film treatment of
ethnic groups and foreign nations, as well as on an intensive recent
examination of films that deal with Mexico, Mexican-Americans,
and Latin America.

Many Mexicos (to borrow a label from Lesley Byrd Simpson)
emerge from Hollywood's textbook.[10] These many Mexicos have
straddled a series of dimensions—geographical, temporal, ethnic,
gender, psychological, and metaphorical. Geographically,
Hollywood's Mexico consists of the U.S.-Mexican border as a
specific region and the rest of Mexico as an undifferentiated mass.
Temporally, there is historical Mexico—usually portrayed with
escapist equanimity—and contemporary Mexico, often treated with
ethnocentric alarm. In terms of ethnicity and gender, Hollywood's
Mexico consists of "greasers" (usually men) and romantic, occasionally sophisticated, sometimes hot-blooded Spaniards (often
women). Psychologically, movie Mexico has alternated between

---

[8]For a discussion of Hollywood's treatment of foreign nations see Siegfried Kracauer,
"National Types as Hollywood Presents Them," in *Public Opinion Quarterly* 13
(Spring 1949), pp. 53-72.
[9]Among the general introductions to the impact of motion pictures on U.S. society
are Robert Sklar, *Movie-Made America: A Cultural History of American Movies* (New
York: Random House, 1975) and Garth Jowett, *Film: The Democratic Art* (Boston:
Little, Brown, 1976).
[10]Lesley Byrd Simpson, *Many Mexicos* (Berkeley: University of California Press, 1941).

being a good neighbor and a neighboring menace. Finally, while Hollywood occasionally treats Mexico as a historical and cultural reality on its own terms, more often it uses Mexico as a metaphor: a backdrop for American activity, a foil for displays of American superiority, a stage on which Americans conduct their own personal morality plays, and sometimes a surrogate for political and ideological struggles within the United States.

GREASERS IN THE SOUTHWEST, REVOLUTION NEXT DOOR

The roots of the Hollywood textbook on Mexico stretch back into the mid-nineteenth century, decades before the advent of motion pictures. The 1846-1848 U.S.-Mexican War catapulted Mexico into the American public consciousness as "the enemy," and American popular culture portrayed Mexico as a particularly inept and cruel enemy, combining the worst aspects of Black Legend Hispanism and savage Indianism.[11]

The war was followed by another cultural phenomenon, the rise of western fiction, which demonstrated its economic and entertainment value through the wide-selling "dime novel." These novels solidified a sure-fire formula, the victory of the Anglo cowboy over those two omnipresent frontier threats, *mexicanos* and Indians.[12] Menacing Mexicans and hostile Indians became a staple of the national public image. With the arrival of flicks at the end of the century, it was natural that the infant movie industry would draw upon this popular western theme. Simultaneously such westerns helped to reinforce public perceptions about Mexicans.

Film titles reflected the pervasiveness and blatancy of this early film theme. Mexicans and Mexican-Americans, often indistinguishable, surfaced in "greaser" movies like *The Greaser's Gauntlet* (1908), *Tony the Greaser* (1911), *The Greaser's Revenge* (1914), and *The Girl and the Greaser* (1915). As one scholar has pointed out, in the early

[11]For an analysis of U.S. mythology about the Mexican War see Robert W. Johannsen, *To the Halls of the Montezumas: The Mexican War in the American Imagination* (Chicago: University of Chicago Press, 1985).
[12]Pettit, *Images of the Mexican American*, pp. 22-44; Cecil Robinson, *With the Ears of Strangers: Mexicans and Mexican Americans in American Literature* (Tucson: University of Arizona Press, 1977), pp. 27-28; and Ralph E. Friar and Natasha A. Friar, *The Only Good Indian... The Hollywood Gospel* (New York: Drama Book Specialists, 1972), pp. 17-68.

days of U.S. motion pictures the *mexicano* served as the "convenient villain,"[13] a role that was shared with the American Indian.[14] Audience reactions reveal that such films may have achieved more than their intended impact. For example, a 1911 issue of *Moving Picture World* reported that audiences responded to the film *Across the Mexican Line* (1911) by hissing the Mexican villain and applauding the actions of Anglos.[15]

Beginning in the 1910s, history gave Hollywood the impetus to broaden its vision from *mexicanos* in the Old West to *mexicanos* in the New West, using the theme of the Mexican Revolution. That explosion next door quickly drew a flood of American filmmakers, to such a degree that one latter-day journalist would label the Revolution "the war waged to make a movie."[16] The Revolution thus became the second basic component of the early *mexicano* film image.[17]

That cycle included *The Mexican Revolutionists* (1912), *Barbarous Mexico* (1913), and *The Mexican Rebellion* (1914). To provide authenticity for its battle scenes, the 1914 feature film *Under Fire in Mexico* even borrowed Mexican federal troops, at that time interned at Eagle Pass, Texas.[18] Some movies lauded the participation of Americans in the Revolution, such as the 1911 *A Prisoner of Mexico*, which showed "General" Francisco Madero riding at the head of his cavalry.

Among Mexican revolutionary figures, Francisco "Pancho" Villa emerged for a while as Hollywood's cult favorite. Villa helped himself by negotiating a $25,000 film contract with Mutual Film Corporation, giving the latter an "exclusive" to cover Villa's

---

[13]Blaine S. Lamb, "The Convenient Villain: The Early Cinema Views the Mexican-American," *Journal of the West* 14:4 (October 1975):75-81.

[14]Friar, *The Only Good Indian*, pp. 69-147, and Gretchen M. Bataille and Charles L. P. Silet, eds., *The Pretend Indians: Images of Native Americans in the Movies* (Ames: Iowa State University Press, 1980).

[15]*Moving Picture World* 8 (27 May 1911), p. 1201, cited in Lamb, "Convenient Villain," pp. 80-81.

[16]David A. Weiss, *Coronet*, February 1952, p. 38, quoted in Kevin Brownlow, *The War, the West and the Wilderness* (New York: Alfred A. Knopf, 1979), p. 87.

[17]More extensive discussions of the U.S. film treatment of the Mexican Revolution can be found in Margarita de Orellana, "La Regard Circulaire: Le Cinéma Américain dans la Révolution Mexicaine (1911-1917)" (Doctoral dissertation, Ecole des Hautes Etudes en Sciences Sociales, Paris, 1982), and Deborah E. Mistron, "The Institutional Revolution: Images of the Mexican Revolution in the Cinema" (Ph.D. dissertation, Indiana University, 1982).

[18]Brownlow, *War*, p. 92.

campaign. (Following Villa's example, General Alvaro Obregón also signed an American film contract.) Villa's agreement also provided that, if necessary, he would schedule battles at times propitious for filming. When Mutual's cameramen were late in arriving to cover his assault on Ojinaga, Villa delayed his attack. Unfortunately, this also gave federal troops time to strengthen their positions.[19] Villa's movie career reached its peak with the 1915 film *The Life of General Francisco Villa*, starring the general himself (he reportedly delayed executions until later in the morning so that cameramen could get better shots of the firing squad and victims in action).[20]

Unlike the image of the villainous greaser of an escapist western past, movie-viewed revolutionary Mexico was becoming an ominous part of the inescapable American present. Sometimes it menaced foreigners who lucklessly stumbled into Mexico, like the unfortunate Anglo in the 1915 movie *Shaved in Mexico*, who makes the mistake of wooing Señorita Hitchey Koo and finds himself the target of vengeance by her Mexican suitor, Señor La Bullio, the irascible town barber. Usually, however, American heroes succeeded in overcoming Mexican obstacles. In the 1915 film *The Lamb*, for example, the great Hollywood adventure star Douglas Fairbanks single-handedly saves a kidnapped American girl from a band of fierce Yaquis who had just whipped a full detachment of Mexican soldiers.

Sometimes the Mexican menace penetrated the United States itself. As the United States was being drawn into World War I, movies warned of a threat coming from the south in such films as *A Mexican Spy in America* (1914) and *The Love Thief* (1916). Or take William Randolph Hearst's 1916-17 serial, *Patria*, which portrayed a Mexican-Japanese alliance to subvert the United Sates, with Mexican and Japanese saboteurs teaming up in an attempt to wreak havoc by blowing up bridges and munitions factories: fortunately, their evil is equaled by their incompetence, and the American heroes thwart their efforts at every turn.[21]

Predictably, American feature films justified U.S. incursions into revolutionary Mexico. *The Insurrection* rationalized the U.S. occupation of Veracruz by asserting that Mexico had been plotting to

---

[19]For a first-person account of a Mutual cameraman's experience with Villa, see Francis A. Collins, *Revolution* (New York: Century, 1916).
[20]Brownlow, *War*, pp. 101-102.
[21]*Variety*, 24 November 1916.

attack the U.S. Caribbean fleet. And the 1916 Universal serial, *Liberty*, informed American audiences that General John J. Pershing had given the Mexicans a sound licking during his expedition into northern Mexico.

By the late 1910s, then, two views of Mexico had become solidified in the pantheon of Hollywood clichés. On an individual level stood the Mexican greaser, a most convenient villain. On the national level stood revolutionary Mexico, a land of chaos and menace, a theme that would be recycled over the decades in films ranging from biographies like *Viva Villa!* (1934) and *Viva Zapata!* (1952) to shoot-em-ups like *They Came to Cordura* (1959), *The Professionals* (1966), and *The Wild Bunch* (1969).

THE MEXICAN GENDER-ETHNICITY GAP

For the most part, cinematic violent Mexicans were men. Occasionally, however, *mexicanas* got in their despicable licks in movies like *The Red Girl* (1908) and *The Love Thief* (1916), in which a *mexicana* revolutionary gunrunner tries to frame an American soldier for murder. But Mexican women generally occupied a more benign film niche, as in *The Mexican Joan of Arc* (1911).

To a degree this gap reflected the ethnic sexual double standard that had become nearly de rigueur for Hollywood movies. This double standard held that filmic interethnic sexual relations between whites and nonwhites (as defined by U.S. racial perceptions) were bad. Should they occur, they must end in failure, even tragedy. That informal guideline became explicit in the 1930 Motion Picture Production Code, better known as the Hays Code, which dominated U.S. films until the mid-1950s and was not officially buried until 1966. The code read, in part, "*Miscegenation* (sex relationship between the white and black races) is forbidden."[22] The application of this filmic "no-no" to white-black, white-Asian, and white-Indian love relationships was reasonably clear and consistent. However, where Mexicans and other Latinos were involved, the diverse, racially mixed nature of Latino ethnicity created both complications and options. So, in the Latino variant it was not proper for male greasers—dark-skinned, usually Indianized

---

[22]From the 1930 Motion Picture Production Code, printed in Robert H. Stanley and Charles S. Steinberg, *The Media Environment: Mass Communications in American Society* (New York: Hastings House, 1976), p. 82.

Mexican or other Latino men—to have love affairs with Anglo women. Yet, as every good Hollywooder knew, Mexican gentlemen prefer blondes, or for that matter any Anglo woman over Mexican women. So in movies the unrestrained sexual lust of swarthy Latinos became a constant threat to Anglo womanhood, a film menace from which Anglo heroes could rescue their damsels, usually in westerns.

But what about the so-called "Latin Lovers"? Ignore them! One of the ironies of interethnic movie history is that, during the silent and early sound eras, such lovers were seldom Latin American characters, but rather were usually Italian or Spanish. Actor Ricardo Cortez was really Jacob Kranz of Austria, while Mexican immigrant film star Ramón Novarro, the archetype Latin lover, played a Frenchman in *Scaramouche*, a Jew in *Ben Hur*, an Austrian in *The Prisoner of Zenda*, and even South Sea chief Motauri in *Where the Pavement Ends*, but he rarely played Latin Americans.

Things changed when genders were reversed, however. While most Latino men could not win the hand of Anglo women (a few light-skinned Spanish-type men did), Anglo men could be successful with Latinas. A giant step for interethnic democracy? Not quite. In most of these cases, the Mexican women turned out to be relatively fair in hue (black hair was acceptable), somewhat cultured (for a Hollywood Latina), and usually of good Spanish or at least Latino elite background. Not just any Mexican woman would do for an Anglo hero, only classy light-skinned *mexicanas*; dark-skinned ones need not apply. For dark *mexicanas* was reserved what would become a traditional Latina niche—prostitution or at least flexible virtue, usually blended with suitably fiery temper (from what Puerto Rican actress Rita Moreno has called the "Yonkee Peeg" school of acting).[23]

Moreover, in keeping with the filmic pattern of asserting Anglo ethnic superiority the Anglo hero usually won the light-skinned Mexican woman from a dark-skinned Mexican man, the standard useful-but-disposable Indianized Mexican greaser.[24] Films set in Mexico or the U.S. Southwest, such as *The Mexican's Revenge* (1909),

---

[23]Jack Hicks, "*9 to 5*'s Rita Moreno: The Cutthroats Almost Got Her," *TV Guide*, 15 January, 1982, p. 28.

[24]This theme is addressed further in Juan Bruce-Novoa, "The Hollywood Americano in Mexico," in *Mexico and the United States: Intercultural Relations in the Humanities*, ed. Juanita Luna Lawhn; Juan Bruce-Novoa; Guillermo Campos; and Ramón Saldívar (San Antonio: San Antonio College, 1984), pp. 22-24.

His Mexican Bride (1909), *The Mexican's Jealousy* (1910), and *Carmenita the Faithful* (1911), carried this message. The Mexican Revolution provided Hollywood with an ideal backdrop for American sexual and military exploits. In the 1914 *The Aztec Treasure*, the American hero leads poor Mexicans in a successful rebellion that topples a repressive provincial governor (mestizo, of course), wins the hand of a local "Spanish" aristocrat, and becomes governor himself. Sometimes out of love for or loyalty to Anglos, *mexicanas* even turned against their own families, as in *Chiquita, the Dancer* (1912). These themes also spread throughout the rest of the Americas, down through Panama in *The Ne'er Do-Well* (1923), to South America in *Argentine Love* (1924), and even to fictitious Latin American nations like Paragonia in *The Americano* (1916).

THE MEXICAN COUNTERATTACK

World War I had a dramatic impact on international movie economics, with important implications for the Mexican film image. During World War I, as European movie production and distribution went into a tailspin, Latin America became an expanding market for U.S. motion pictures. Following the war, with Hollywood now hooked on Latin American movie receipts, Mexico led a hemispheric challenge to Hollywood's negative stereotyping of Latinos.

In 1919, Mexico sent a formal protest to American filmmakers, accusing them of emphasizing Mexico's worst aspects and threatening to restrict them from working in Mexico. When this approach failed, the Mexican government issued a ban on all movies that presented derogatory portrayals of Mexicans and threatened to prohibit all American movies if Hollywood did not drop its "greaser" approach. According to one Mexican government official, "ill will toward Mexico has been inflamed by these pictures to such an extent that the Mexican government found it necessary to make such a protest."[25] Other Latin American nations followed Mexico's lead. As late as 1931, Brazil protested against *Rio's Road*

---

[25]*New York Times*, 11 February 1922, p. 15, quoted in Allen L. Woll, "Bandits and Lovers: Hispanic Images in American Film," in *The Kaleidoscopic Lens: How Hollywood Views Ethnic Groups*, ed. Randall M. Miller (Englewood, N.J.: Jerome S. Ozer, 1980), pp. 56-57.

to Hell (1931) and Cuba banned all MGM films after that studio released *Cuban Love Song* (1931).[26]

This strategy worked to a degree, although it failed to achieve consistent results. Following the Mexican government's original ban, for example, Famous Players-Lasky, which had just signed a deal to distribute one hundred movies in Mexico, issued a statement that "the wishes of the Mexican government would be respected."[27] In the export version of *Girl of the Golden West* (1930), all scenes with Mexican bandits were eliminated. At times movie Mexicans demonstrated courage, as in *The Mark of Zorro* (1920) and *Senor Daredevil* (1926), and occasionally Hollywood even showed some sensitivity to the plight of Mexicans and Mexican-Americans, as in the various filmings of Helen Hunt Jackson's novel *Ramona* (for example, 1928 and 1936).

After the 1918 *Guns and Greasers*, the greaser disappeared from movie titles but not from all movies. Hollywood did not want to totally bury the Latino villains who had proven to be great box office in the United States, so studios came up with various approaches. For example, Hollywood invented fictitious but obviously Latino nations such as Costa Roja in *The Dove* (1928), which had no government that could lodge a protest.

The 1932 film *The Girl of the Río* demonstrated that Latin America might win battles, but the image war would go on and on. *The Girl of the Río* featured Leo Carrillo as the drunken, despicable hoodlum, Señor Tostado, one of the most unsavory and sadistic greasers yet to reach the screen. The movie generated possibly the most concerted and unified pan-Hispanic response ever mounted. Mexico banned the film first, followed by Panama and Nicaragua. Spain and other Latin American nations joined the protest through a series of reciprocal treaties banning films that "attacked, slandered, defamed, insulted or misrepresented" Hispanics and threatened an embargo on *all* films from companies that fostered that negative image.[28]

---

[26]Allen L. Woll, *The Latin Image in American Film* (Los Angeles: Latin American Center, University of California, 1977), pp. 16-18, 34.
[27]*New York Times*, 3 January 1928, p. 28, quoted in Woll, "Bandits and Lovers," p. 57.
[28]League of Nations, *Treaty Series*, vol. 165 (1935), no. 3818, quoted in Woll, "Bandits and Lovers," p. 58.

Once again Hollywood backed off. In films about Mexico, evil and lust began to give way to music, romance, and silliness. For example, Hollywood now entertained American audiences with *Captain Thunder, Hot Tamale Breaker* (1931), and *The Kid from Spain* (1932), in which an American expatriate (Eddie Cantor) masquerades as a torero and manages to calm a fighting bull by repeating the magic word Po-po-CA-te-PET-tl.

This changing emphasis also had an impact on the gender gap, which would develop through the 1930s. In contrast to previous decades, the lot of Latino men seemed to improve, with some of them—particularly Mexican historical heros—receiving at least semiserious treatment. But Latinas, if anything, were taken even less seriously than before.[29]

Two Mexican actresses—Dolores Del Río and Lupe Vélez— became important screen personalities of the 1930s. Yet both experienced career frustrations due to their *mexicanismo*. The coolly sensual Del Río seldom found screen roles to match her talent. Becoming frustrated with the superficiality of the Latina characters she was asked to play, she left Hollywood in 1943 and returned to Mexico, where she won four Ariels, the Mexican equivalent of the Academy Award.

Del Río's refined coolness contrasted with the hot screen sensuality of Lupe Vélez. At first Vélez became one of Hollywood's leading all-purpose ethnics, playing, in her own words, "Chinese, Eskimos, Japs, squaws, Hindus, Swedes, Malays, and Javanese."[30] Ultimately she became known as the Mexican Spitfire, a sobriquet drawn from her 1939 film of the same name and its various sequels, including the *Mexican Spitfire's Elephant* (1942).

Like Vélez and Del Río, glamorous Mexican immigrant actress Raquel Torres played a variety of Latin and other exotic ethnic roles in films ranging from *White Shadows of the South Seas* (1928) to *The Bridge at San Luis Rey* (1929) to *Aloha* (1931). From out of Brazil came the high-voltage Carmen Miranda. Confined to frivolous roles, she is best remembered for her bizarre headdresses, hotly rhythmed

---

[29]For a more extensive discussion of the image of Latinas in U.S. films see Carlos E. Cortés, "Chicanas in Film: History of an Image," in *Chicano Cinema: Research, Reviews, and Resources*, ed. Gary D. Keller (Binghamton, N.Y.: Bilingual Review/Press, 1985), pp. 94-108.

[30]*Saturday Evening Post*, 2 January 1932, p. 26, cited in Woll, *The Latin Image*, p. 38.

Latin songs, and heavily accented English. Melodies and love had superseded violence and villainly in Hollywood's Latin American textbook.

THE GOOD NEIGHBOR POLICY

The 1932 presidential election of Franklin D. Roosevelt led to the establishment of the Latin American Good Neighbor Policy. Hollywood was urged to play an important role. Reflecting this new orientation toward Latin America, Hollywood began to mine Mexican history, although often using it merely as a backdrop for Anglo heroism and American morality plays.

The Mexican Revolution had been a hot contemporary movie topic during the 1910s, but Mexican history had seldom attracted Hollywood filmmakers. A notable exception was Cecil B. DeMille's 1917 mini-epic, *The Woman God Forgot*, which told the story of Cortés and Moctezuma.[31] During the 1930s, however, Mexican history crept into American movies, although the results were often ludicrous.

Hollywood could not resist comic book treatment of Mexican history. The Mexican romantic hero Zorro righted wrongs with daring and intelligence, but his films shredded history as he shredded villains. For example, the 1939 Republic Pictures serial, *Zorro's Fighting Legion*, proclaimed Benito Juárez to be Mexico's first president in 1824, more than three decades before he actually took office.[32] That era's other major Mexican film hero, the Cisco Kid, became little more than a galloping, charming stick figure in such movies as *Cisco Kid and the Lady* (1939), *Return of the Cisco Kid* (1939), *Lucky Cisco Kid* (1940), and *Viva Cisco Kid* (1940).

Hollywood's supposedly serious movies also tended to lacerate history. In the 1933 *The Man from Monterey*, John Wayne comes to the rescue of post-Treaty of Guadalupe Hidalgo annexed Mexicans, convincing them to register their land grants with the U.S. government against the opposition of some unscrupulous Mexicans. The film left the impression that Wayne saved the day for these new Mexican-Americans. Of course it did not address the long-range aftermath, in which most annexed Mexicans ultimately lost their land grants.

---

[31]*Variety*, 2 November 1917, p. 49.
[32]Emilio García Riera, "En la frontera de México fue ...," *Dicine* 1:4 (January 1984):7.

Hollywood did make some goodwill gestures to Mexico in its historical films, although these gestures were often ineffectual and sometimes even cynical. MGM obtained Mexican government script approval before filming its 1934 pseudo-biography *Viva Villa!*, although one would never know this from viewing the violent, ludicrously macho final product, which was banned in Mexico. The character of Villa improved somewhat in later filmic re-creations, such as *Villa!* (1958) and *Villa Rides* (1968), although history continued to take a beating.

In contrast, despite its historical inaccuracies, the 1939 film biography *Juárez* at least reflected efforts to provide a more serious examination of Mexico. Yet even here Hollywood transformed the celebration of the renowned nineteenth-century Mexican president, Benito Juárez, into dutiful obeisance to U.S. role modeling. Whose picture hung omnipresently behind the Mexican president as he moved his government around the country while being pursued by French troops? None other than Abraham Lincoln.

Furthermore, Juárez functions greatly as a spokesman for anti-Hitler Hollywood, with Napoleon III and Maximilian serving as unsubtle metaphors for Hitler. As the symbol of patriotic resistance against European aggression, Juárez intones, in perfect Monroe Doctrine rhetoric, "By what right, señores, do the great powers of Europe invade the lands of simple people ...? The world must know the fate of any usurper who sets his foot on this soil." (Juárez was not movie Mexico's only anti-Hitlerian surrogate. In the 1937 *The Bold Caballero*, Zorro defeats the corrupt "Austrian" commandant of Spanish northern California.) While Juárez emerges as a political hero, the film does less well by him in human terms. The movie's rigid, humorless, vengeance-bound Zapotec Indian comes out a poor second to the personable, well-intended but poorly counseled Emperor Maximilian, so that the latter's death provides the film's final tragedy. In rejecting appeals to show mercy and spare the life of the sympathetic Maximilian, Juárez becomes the ultimate greaser, an avenging Indian with political power.[33]

Then came World War II. Once the United States entered the war, Latin America's strategic importance prompted the U.S. government to encourage Hollywood to be an even better neighbor.

---

[33]Paul Vanderwood, "Introduction: A Political Barometer," in *Juárez*, ed. P. Vanderwood (Madison: University of Wisconsin Press, 1983), pp. 9-41.

The U.S. Office of the Coordinator of Inter-American Affairs, under Director Nelson Rockefeller, stressed the need for U.S. motion pictures to help solidify the Americas in the common struggle against the Axis powers. The Hays Office, Hollywood's official self-censor, appointed a Latin American expert to help Hollywood avoid filmic blunders that might offend Latin Americans.[34] Even Walt Disney joined the war effort, producing two animated salutes to the United States' hemispheric neighbors, *Saludos Amigos* (1943) and *The Three Caballeros* (1945). While these films embody just about every imaginable silly Latino stereotype, at least they reflect a friendly if not always respectful vision of Latin American life and culture.

Hollywood turned into a military recruiter, calling upon all Americans, including Mexican-Americans, to fight for their country. In wartime-made World War II films, Chicanos fought and died alongside their Anglo comrades. In fact, Hollywood's wartime "affirmative action" policy was to assign a variety of "recognizable" ethnic characters, often including a Chicano, to each movie military unit in order to demonstrate all-American togetherness. Even in the traditional western genre, where Mexicans had been greasers, villains, buffoons or, at best, comic strip heros, they now sometimes emerged as serious characters, even victims of Anglo prejudice, as in *The Ox-Bow Incident* (1943), where "The Mexican," as he is called throughout the film, becomes one of the innocent victims of a lynching.

RISE OF THE BORDER, RETURN OF THE BANDIDO

Progress had been made. The end of World War II, however, brought a decline of U.S. government interest in Latin America and ended Hollywood's Good Neighbor Policy. Thereafter, Latinos appeared less frequently in films and the picture was mixed when they did appear.

Filled with the crusading euphoria of the war years, early postwar Hollywood produced a flood of films attacking prejudice and discrimination against various ethnic groups. Eric Johnston, president of the Motion Picture Association, proclaimed that "the motion picture, as an instrument for the promotion of knowledge

---

[34]Woll, *The Latin Image*, pp. 54-56.

and understanding among peoples, stands on the threshold of a tremendous era of expansion."[35] Films like *A Medal for Benny* (1945), *The Lawless* (1950), *The Ring* (1952), *Trial* (1955), and *Giant* (1956) criticized prejudice and discrimination against Mexican-Americans. Movie social criticism also began to address a new issue, the exploitation of undocumented workers, in films such as *Border Incident* (1949) and *Wetbacks* (1956). In most of these films *mexicanos* served mainly as passive pawns, the background for Anglo conflict, but there were exceptions. In *Border Incident*, for example, Ricardo Montalbán plays an intelligent and courageous Mexican government agent who poses as an undocumented worker and attempts to break up a smuggling ring. Yet, as could have been predicted from Hollywood's tradition of Anglo superiority, Montalbán dies in the line of duty while his Anglo law enforcement counterpart nabs the villains.

Interestingly, the theme of undocumented immigration was emerging simultaneously in Mexican films.[36] In most of these movies, Mexicans decide to go to the United States to find a better life, only to return defeated. To a great extent these films ignored the Mexican socioeconomic conditions that propelled emigrants north and made fun of their misadventures, portraying emigrants as cultural bumblers in a more "advanced" society. Rare were films like Alejandro Galindo's 1953 *Espaldas mojadas*, which dealt seriously with the theme of emigration and treated the Mexican protagonists with a sense of dignity and even heroism.[37]

If Mexican movies generally scorned undocumented immigrants they heaped opprobrium on *pochos*, whose experience in the United States had tainted their Mexican purity, a loss that becomes apparent when they return to Mexico. Some movies went so far as to treat them as traitors. These themes pervaded such films as *Primero soy mexicano* (1950), *Acá las tortas* (1951), and *Soy mexicano de acá de este lado* (1951).[38] The undocumented immigrant films also reflected the growth of both U.S. and Mexican film interest in the

---

[35]Eric C. Johnston, "The Right to Know," *Motion Picture Letter* (Public Information Committee of the Motion Picture Industry) 5:6 (June 1946).

[36]The most comprehensive English-language analysis of the history of Mexican motion pictures is Carl Mora's *Mexican Cinema: Reflections of a Society, 1896-1980* (Berkeley: University of California Press, 1982).

[37]David R. Maciel, "Visions of the Other Mexico: Chicanos and Undocumented Workers in Mexican Cinema, 1954-1982," in *Chicano Cinema: Research, Reviews, and Resources, pp. 82-84.*

[38]Norma Iglesias, *La visión de la frontera a través del cine mexicano* (Tijuana: Centro de Estudios Fronterizos del Norte de México, 1985), pp. 11-12.

theme of the U.S.-Mexican border. The border had periodically played a role in Hollywood film, as in the 1935 *Bordertown*, although it generally had served as a relatively neutral background. In Hollywood's new vision, however, the border was no longer neutral but now threatened Americans.

The iconic film of this new wave was Orson Welles's chilling 1958 classic, *Touch of Evil*, set in fictional twin cities on the U.S.-Mexican border. Predictably, the Mexican town emerges as the source of every imaginable type of corruption. However, the film reversed two Hollywood traditions: First, the hero, Mexican narcotics agent Mike Vargas (Charlton Heston), uses intelligence and courage to defeat the corrupt Anglo sheriff (Welles). Second, Vargas has a white, blond American wife (Janet Leigh). Welles had indeed broken through some Hollywood barriers. Other Hollywood films presented a similarly noxious vision of border Mexico, but without Welles's brilliance and defiance of Hollywood traditions of Anglo superiority. Filled with danger, reeking of vice, Hollywood's border Mexico was truly the menace next door. Unfortunately for border Mexico, its made-in-Hollywood decadent image was mirrored in Mexican films made predominantly, of course, by Mexico City filmmakers. For these filmmakers, the border existed principally as a den of crime and prostitution, with Ciudad Juárez receiving special attention. *Cruel destino* (1943), *La herencia de la llorona* (1946), and *Frontera norte* (1953) embodied this vision of northern Mexico from the Mexican capital.[39]

Paralleling the rise of the border film came Hollywood's resurrection of the Mexican bandido, in all of his swarthy treachery and savagery, combined with the reassertion of Anglo-American superiority. Ironically, these themes stand out in what is probably the finest American film ever set in Mexico, the late John Huston's *The Treasure of the Sierra Madre* (1947), one of the all-time great motion pictures. The prototype of the "new greaser" was embodied in actor Alfonso Bedoya, who resurrected the vicious bandido film legacy with his remarkable portrayal of Gold Tooth, a sadistic Mexican bandit who machetes Humphrey Bogart to death and then scatters Bogart's bags of gold dust, stupidly mistaking it for sand.[40] Simultaneously, old American prospector Walter Huston

---

[39]Ibid., pp. 9-11.
[40]For an analysis of Alfonso Bedoya's portrayal of Gold Tooth see James Naremore, "Introduction: A Likely Project," in *The Treasure of the Sierra Madre*, ed. J. Naremore (Madison: University of Wisconsin Press, 1979), p. 28.

becomes a nearly god-like hero to a village of Mexican Indians, as he saves a young drowning victim with artificial respiration ("an old Boy Scout trick," he says). The village responds in gratitude by making him its honored guest, presumably for life.

After *Treasure*, the Mexican bandido once again became fair game in films like *Ride, Vaquero!* (1953), *The Magnificent Seven* (1960), and *The Outrage* (1964), a spurious westernization of the Japanese classic *Rashomon*. The Mexican bandido eventually became an international staple, particularly in Italy, where director Sergio Leone made him a fixture (along with Clint Eastwood) in such so-called spaghetti westerns as *A Fistful of Dollars* (1967), *For a Few Dollars More* (1967), and *The Good, the Bad, and the Ugly* (1969). Even Mexican movies joined the chorus in Mexican westerns, often set on the U.S.-Mexican border, and in *comedias rancheras*. According to Chicano filmmaker Jesús Treviño, these films featured the traditional Hollywood western stereotypes, with Mexicans appearing "de bigote, con sombrero y carrilleras, siempre sucios y deprabados y con botella de tequila en la mano."[41]

MEXICAN HISTORY REVISITED

Mexican history continued to attract Hollywood filmmakers, although the results could hardly meet scholarly standards of accuracy and cultural validity. Mayan Indians are pseudoanthropologically mangled in *Kings of the Sun* (1963). Cortés conquers Mexico once more in *Captain from Castile* (1947). Texas again wins its freedom in *The Alamo* (1960). Colonel John Fremont's Anglo pioneers capture northern California from Mexico in *California Conquest* (1952), aided by a local "Spanish" rancher (Fremont gives an encore in the 1986 television mini-series *Dream West*). Mexico defeats the French in *Vera Cruz* (1954) and again in *Major Dundee* (1964), while the Mexican Revolution returns with *The Fugitive* (1948), *Viva Zapata!* (1952), *They Came to Cordura* (1959), and *Villa Rides* (1968). On the surface, this attention to Mexican history seemed to be a continuation of the Good Neighbor Policy. In fact, the structure of most of these historical films provided a reassertion of the theme of Anglo dominance and the continuing manipulation of Mexican history to address American moral dilemmas and political concerns.

---

[41]Jesús Treviño, "Presencia del cine chicano," in *A través de la frontera* (Mexico City: Instituto de Investigaciones Estéticas, Universidad Nacional de México, 1983), p. 195.

They Came to Cordura deals less with Mexican history than with the meaning of personal bravery, as displayed when Pershing's 1917 U.S. army expeditionary force defeats Pancho Villa's army in a film battle which, of course, never really occurred. (Mexico banned the film after it was shown there briefly, but time appears to have lessened its sting and the movie now appears occasionally on Mexican television.) In *Villa Rides*, it takes the daring bombing attacks of an audacious American pilot to transform potential villista defeats into glorious victories.

While *Vera Cruz* portrays the *juaristas* as brave patriots battling the French occupiers, it also bestows principal credit for the Mexican victory on an avaricious American outlaw (Burt Lancaster) and a former Confederate officer (Gary Cooper). In *Major Dundee*, Union and Confederate soldiers put aside their antagonisms in order to ride into Mexico and defeat the French. So it should come as no surprise if American moviegoers, generally ignorant of Mexican history, concluded that Americans led the way in eliminating the French intervention.

Emiliano Zapata followed Villa into the Hollywood revolutionary pantheon in the engrossing, if historically flawed, *Viva Zapata!* (1952), directed by Elia Kazan from a screenplay by John Steinbeck. On one level, the film remains one of the most positive portrayals of Mexico in American film history. While it offers plenty of villains (a cold, ruthless Victoriano Huerta) and weaklings (a detached, indecisive Francisco Madero), it also features a decent and courageous peasantry imbued with Jeffersonian agrarian values and, of course, a heroic, humane, and dedicated Emiliano Zapata, whom most American viewers could applaud.

However, *Viva Zapata!* has given rise to varying and conflicting interpretations.[42] Historian Paul Vanderwood sees the movie Zapata as a "Cold War warrior," the Kazan-Steinbeck surrogate for their own anticommunist stance during the Hollywood civil war over suspected communist infiltration of the industry, a war detonated by the terror tactics of the House Un-American Activities Committee.[43] According to Vanderwood's intriguing and

---

[42]For an Indianist interpretation of *Viva Zapata!* see Carroll Britch and Cliff Lewis, "Shadow of the Indian in the Fiction of John Steinbeck," *MELUS* 11:2 (summer 1984):39-58.

[43]Paul Vanderwood, "An American Cold Warrior: *Viva Zapata!*" in *American History/American Film: Interpreting the Hollywood Image*, ed. John E. O'Connor and Martin A. Jackson (New York: Frederick Ungar, 1979), pp. 183-201. For a personal interpretation of that Hollywood civil war see Victor Navasky, *Naming Names* (New York: Viking Press, 1980).

compelling Cold War interpretation, Zapata (Marlon Brando) stands as the bulwark of democratic, anticommunist purity as he resists the seductive opportunism of the subversive totalitarian Fernando Aguirre (Joseph Wiseman). A contrary interpretation comes from Robert Morsberger in his introduction to the published screenplay of *Viva Zapata!*[44] Morsberger sees the film as an extension of Steinbeck's long-time literary opposition to totalitarianism of the left and right and his championing of the little guy, especially the agricultural little guy. In response to attacks on the film from various points on the ideological spectrum, Kazan wrote, "there was, of course, no such thing as a Communist Party at the time and place where Zapata fought .... But there is such a thing as a Communist mentality. We created a figure of this complexion in Fernando," who "typifies the men who use the just grievances of the people for their own ends, who shift and twist their course, betray any friend or principle or promise to get power and keep it."[45]

Postrevolutionary Mexico became the focus of U.S. movie attention in John Ford's *The Fugitive* (1948). Based on Graham Greene's novel *The Power and the Glory*, the film deals with persecution of Catholic priests in Tabasco. In making this powerful though historically flawed film, director John Ford used an all-Mexican crew and an almost entirely Mexican cast, including the Mexican repatriate actress Dolores Del Río.

One final, notable Mexican aspect of the postwar movie era was the reversal of the prewar gender gap. In contrast to the bubble-headed prewar señoritas, the postwar era gave rise to strong, intelligent, resourceful screen *mexicanas*. *One-Eyed Jacks* (1961) featured impressive characterizations by Katy Jurado and Pina Pellicer as a Mexican-American mother and her daughter. In Stanley Kramer's memorable 1952 western, *High Noon*, the intelligent *mexicana*, Helen Ramírez, is both a powerful commercial force in the hypocritical town and an insightful moral interpreter as she provides a cram course on frontier values for the wife of the besieged town marshal. In the 1953 underground classic *Salt of the Earth*, brave and resolute Chicanas lead the way to a labor victory against

---

[44]Robert E. Morsberger, "Steinbeck's Zapata: Rebel versus Revolutionary," in *Viva Zapata! The Original Screenplay*, by John Steinbeck, ed. R. Morsberger (New York: Viking Press, 1975), pp. xi–xxxviii.
[45]Elia Kazan, "Letters to the Editor," *Saturday Review* 35 (25 April 1952):22, quoted in Morsberger, "Steinbeck's Zapata," p. xxx.

a New Mexico mining company, going on the picket line when their striking husbands are barred by court injunction. Ironically, this growth in strong *mexicana* characters occurred precisely at a time when Anglo female characters had entered a period of decline, as the rise of the family film was putting screen women back in their place: the home.[46]

On the other hand, many of these strong *mexicana* female characters were prostitutes, kept women, or ladies of questionable virtue (at least for that era). From Chihuahua (Linda Darnell) in *My Darling Clementine* (1946) to Claire Quintana (Lena Horne) in *Death of a Gunfighter* (1969), the *mexicana* prostitute served as a regular feature of the American western.[47] So while filmdom had elevated *mexicanas* to more prominent, forceful, active roles, Hollywood tempered that image with a heavy dose of moral censure.

THE EVIL NEXT DOOR, THE ANGLO TRIUMPHANT

Even these modest gains have been washed away, beginning in the 1960s. During the past three decades, Mexico and the rest of Latin America have suffered severe setbacks in their Hollywood-influenced public image. Three basic themes have dominated: the first has been the resurgence, with a vengeance and a women's liberation variation, of the theme of Anglo superiority over Mexicans and other Latin Americans. The second has been the portrait of a nearly pathological Latin America, whose decadence and subhumanity pose a threat to Anglos who stumble into the south-of-the-border Hades. Often these two themes are combined, with Anglos emerging victorious, singed but not permanently scarred. The third has been the rise of the Latino menace within the United States.

The neo-Anglo superiority cycle was kicked off in the 1950s with films like *Vera Cruz* and *The Magnificent Seven* (1960). In the latter, an adaptation of Akiro Kurosawa's *Seven Samurai*, seven Americans (two are Chicanos) save a poor Mexican village by wiping out an entire Mexican bandit troop, led by the ominous Calvera, with the loss of only four of the seven magnificents.

---

[46]Marjorie Rosen, *Popcorn Venus. Women, Movies and the American Dream* (New York: Coward, McCann and Geoghegan, 1973), pp. 263-265.
[47]A related analysis of the *mexicana* "fallen woman" can be found in Pettit, *Images of the Mexican American*, pp. 203-207.

So successful was this classy, crisply made flick that it unfortunately earned three ripoff potboiler sequels. Their only element of special interest occurs in the 1968 *Guns of the Magnificent Seven*, when a young lad named Emiliano Zapata observes and becomes inspired by the *americanos* to dedicate himself to improving the lives of poor Mexicans.

It had taken seven magnificents to rout a Mexican outlaw band. By 1966, in *The Professionals*, it takes only four Americans (one black) to liberate a girl from the clutches of a *villista* military encampment, this time without a single casualty. In 1969, a lone black American lawman leads a force of Yaqui rebels to victory over an oppressive Mexican army in *100 Rifles*. That same year, in *The Wild Bunch*, four Anglo outlaws wipe out an entire Mexican army force, although the four "heroes" also die in the process. That Mexican force is led by the sadistic General Mapache (played by Emilio Fernández), who ranks alongside Leo Carrillo's Señor Tostado in *The Girl of the Río* and Alfonso Bedoya's Gold Tooth in *Sierra Madre* as the personification of the special Mexican screen combination of evil and incompetence. Even a bumbling Anglo amateur (Warren Oates) manages to lay waste to a large portion of a Mexican *hacendado*'s private gang before being killed in *Bring Me the Head of Alfredo García* (1974).[48]

This style of asserting Anglo superiority has become so ingrained in the American psyche that it can now be drawn upon for parody. For example, in the 1986 *Three Amigos*, three Anglo movie actors save a small 1916 Mexican town by whipping the villainous El Guapo and his outlaw band. Only occasionally do *mexicanos* from either side of the border demonstrate superiority or even equality to their American adversaries, as in the case of the relentless Chicano Sheriff Bob Valdez, whose rough-hewn intelligence, fighting skills, and perseverance lead to a triumph over a cruel Anglo landowner in the 1971 western *Valdez Is Coming*.

In this era of purported gender equality, it is only natural that Anglo women, too, should demonstrate their superiority over Mexicans. In the 1979 *Sunburn*, Farah Fawcett-Majors leads a group of bumbling Mexican criminals on an interminable car chase through Acapulco before they are able to capture her. In the 1983

---

[48]A more extensive discussion of *Major Dundee, The Wild Bunch,* and *Bring Me the Head of Alfredo García* can be found in Reynold Humphries, "The Function of Mexico in Peckinpah's Films," *Jump Cut* 18 (1978):17-20.

Losin' It, an alienated Anglo housewife (Shelley Long) and a group of Anglo teenage boys stumble into evil Tijuana but manage to escape with their lives by outwitting and outdriving both a gang of young Tijuana toughs and the corrupt local sheriff.

Losin' It also fits into the ongoing picture of Mexican border depravity. Frontier Mexico, especially Tijuana, has become the convenient Hollywood source of background sin and menace. Simultaneously, the Mexican film industry has increased its sensationalistic and often degrading commercialization of Mexican border life. In her provocative monograph *La visión de la frontera a través del cine mexicano*, Norma Iglesias of Tijuana's Centro de Estudios Fronterizos del Norte de México identified 172 "películas fronterizas" in just 1984 and 1985.[49]

The themes of Mexican decadence and threatening ambience pervade other films, like *The Children of Sánchez* (1982), *Against All Odds* (1984), and *Under the Volcano* (1984), which the Mexican newspaper *Excélsior* called "a humiliating vision of Mexico," despite the fact that it was co-produced by the Mexican government.[50] In *Against All Odds* a Mayan temple, in which losing athletic teams had been sacrificed, provides the ominous site for the life-and-death struggle between two Anglo professional football players. Even the laudable *El Norte* (1984), Chicano filmmaker Gregory Nava's sensitive and moving portrayal of Guatemalan immigration to the United States, reinforces the image of Mexican hostility, this time against their Latino brothers and sisters from the south who must traverse the peril-laden human minefield of Mexico in order to reach the promised land of the United States.

In this context, the inept and foolish contemporary Mexican general of *Viva Max!* (1969) seems like a breath of fresh air. True, he embodies silliness and misdirected patriotism when, on his own, he leads his army across the border into contemporary San Antonio and recaptures the Alamo for Mexico. Yet, for all of his foolishness, at least he demonstrates courage and imagination, while his absurdity is exceeded by a cowardly Texas paramilitary unit that tries and fails to recapture the mission. At the end, Max and his troops march proudly out of San Antonio to the cheers of the crowd.

[49]Iglesias, *Visión de la frontera*, p. 4.
[50]Quoted in Concepción Badillo, "'Under Volcano' Draws Irate Reactions in Mexico," *Los Angeles Times*, 14 May 1985.

The rest of Latin America fares no better than Mexico, as a flood of films have turned Latin America into a source of menace and derision unrivaled since the silent era.[51] One can hardly imagine how the cloddish Fidel Castro of *Che!* (1969) could have led a successful revolution and remained head of Cuba for more than a quarter of a century. Yet he is a model of efficiency and effectiveness when compared to the incompetent Bolivian army of *Butch Cassidy and the Sundance Kid* (1969). And what can be said about the ludicrous Latin Americans of *Bananas* (1971), *The In-Laws* (1979), and even *Romancing the Stone* (1984), in which yet another Anglo woman physically triumphs over a Latino macho man, killing the evil Colombian Colonel Zolo in one-on-one combat, although admittedly he is disadvantaged because his hand has just been snapped off by a crocodile? On a more serious note, there are the cruel, corrupt, and decadent Latin Americans of *Sorcerer* (1977) and *Salvador* (1986), and the repressive fascist dictatorships of *Missing* (1982), *Under Fire* (1983), and *Beyond the Limit* (1983). In short, according to recent Hollywood films, not only is Latin America a lousy place to live, but you wouldn't even want to visit there.[52]

THE MENACE WITHIN

The current era has injected one final negative variation to the overall Mexican image. Not only is the Mexican evil next door, but it is also becoming a growing menace within the contemporary United States itself. In some respects this exportation of evil has taken the form of fantasy, as in *Q* (1982), in which ersatz Aztec religion and rituals become fused with science fiction as an excuse for a bloody King Kong-style showdown between a winged serpent (Quetzalcoatl, believe it or not) and the police atop New York City's towering Chrysler Building. While obviously science fiction escapism, *Q* metaphorically recalls the more ominous realistic film treatments of the internal Hispanic menace.

---

[51]These films make a mockery of the prediction of *Time* film critic Richard Schickel, who in 1975 wrote, "Certainly it would be out of the question to make a movie in which whites are seen to do if not just, then justifiable, battle with persons of a non-Caucasian persuasion. If such conflicts are ever again seen on screen they will be used to 'prove' that we—the whites—have been, since the beginning of time, in every clime, genocidal in our racism." See Richard Schickel, "Why Indians Can't Be Villains Any More," *New York Times*, 9 February 1975.

[52]For a discussion of the broader issue of contemporary films about the Third World, see John Powers, "Saints and Savages," *American Film* 9:4 (January-February 1984):38-43.

Movies have returned to an older theme, the problem of Mexican undocumented workers. In some films the smuggling of immigrants provides the basic circumstances, as in *Blood Barrier* (1979), *Borderline* (1980), and *The Border* (1982). And like their 1940s/1950s filmic predecessors, the main screen role of undocumented *mexicanos* is to be passive while Anglos save the day.

Other films have broken new thematic ground for Hollywood, addressing the experience and impact of undocumented workers in the United States. Only rarely does this theme receive serious and sensitive treatment however, as in Robert Young's 1977 *Alambrista!* and in Gregory Nava's 1984 *El Norte*.[53] *El Norte* is also interesting because it addresses a growing American paranoia, the fear that undocumented Mexican immigrants are undermining the U.S. economy by stealing jobs from Americans, a concern that has divided even the Mexican-American community. In *El Norte*, angry because an ambitious young Guatemalan has been promoted over him, a Chicano turns the undocumented immigrant over to *la migra* (the U.S. Immigration and Naturalization Service).

Unfortunately, the theme of economic threat and job displacement seldom receives such serious examination. Usually it is merely injected gratuitously, as in the 1983 sexploitation comedy *My Tutor*, in which two Chicano college students pose as Spanish-speaking undocumented immigrants in order to get maid and gardener jobs at a sumptuous Los Angeles mansion. Whether treated seriously, gratuitously, or subtextually, it is likely that these films have an impact on American viewers by reiterating the themes of undocumented workers as economic threats, especially to Americans seeking jobs.

Finally, a new and even more virulent U.S. Latino presence has taken its place on the screen: the Latino urban gang. Unlike the threat of Mexico, physically distant across the border, or the traditional Mexican bandido, operating at a temporal distance in the escapist past, movie Latino urban gangs strut near and now. Most common have been youth gangs: nationally unspecified Latino gangs in *Bad Boys* (1983); Chicano gangs in *Walk Proud* (1979) and *Boulevard Nights* (1979); and Puerto Rican gangs in *The Young Savages* (1961), *Night of the Juggler* (1980), *Fort Apache, The Bronx* (1981) and, with musical accompaniment, *West Side Story* (1961). Young

---

[53]A provocative assessment of *Alambrista!* is Gregg Barrios, "*Alambrista!* A Modern Odyssey," in *Chicano Cinema: Research, Reviews and Resources*, pp. 165-167.

Chicano hoods have even gained entry into soft pornography, like the title role burglar-turned-corpse-peddler of the cult comedy *Eating Raoul* (1982).

Even more ominous is the wave of movie Latino drug dealers. The past few years alone have given us Latino drug lords in such films as *Code of Silence* (1985), *Stick* (1985), *Stand Alone* (1986), *Running Scared* (1986), and *8 Million Ways to Die* (1986). This movie model was solidified in Brian De Palma's 1983 *Scarface*, which portrayed Cuban-Americans as the ultimate in cocaine-snorting, drug-smuggling, murderous Latinos. So vicious was this portrait that its makers appended the following, ineffective postscript to the movie:

> *Scarface* is the fictional account of the activities of a small group of ruthless criminals. The characters do not represent the Cuban American community and it would be erroneous and unfair to suggest that they do. The vast majority of Cuban Americans have demonstrated a dedication, vitality and enterprise that has enriched the American scene.

The *Scarface*-style Latino has also become a staple of television, though television fiction has generally ignored Mexico per se except as an occasional backdrop for adventures or mysteries. U.S. Hispanics receive somewhat more attention, with generally depressing results. After studying the portrayal of Hispanics in network fictional television series from 1975 to 1978, Bradley S. Greenberg and Pilar Baptista-Fernández reported that television Hispanics fell almost entirely into three categories—law breakers, law enforcers, and comic characters—with "crook" as the most prevalent Hispanic vocation. In fact, two-thirds of all Hispanic characters in television dramatic series (as contrasted with comedy series) were engaged in either law breaking or law enforcing, both areas which involve the use or threat of violence.[54]

A study released in summer 1987 indicated that during the past three decades Hispanics made up only one percent of the educated professionals and business executives portrayed on television.[55]

---

[54]Bradley S. Greenberg and Pilar Baptista-Fernández, "Hispanic-Americans—The New Minority on Television," in *Life on Television: Content Analysis of U.S. TV Drama*, by B. Greenberg et al. (Norwood, New Jersey: Ablex, 1980), pp. 3-12.
[55]S. Robert Lichter, Linda S. Lichter, Stanley Rothman, and Daniel Amundson, "Prime-time Prejudice: TV's Images of Blacks and Hispanics," *Public Opinion* (July-August 1987):16.

Shows that focus on Mexican-American life, whether Chicanos trying to integrate with humorous results in *Condo* or Chicanos living in cultural enclaves in *AKA Pablo*, have not drawn enthusiastic audience responses.[56] Mexican-Americans and Mexico, at most, have remained a fictional television sideshow.

A NEW ERA?

It may be that we are entering a new era. U.S. Latinos now star as admirable Hispanic characters in television dramatic series: Edward James Olmos as stalwart, astute police lieutenant Martin Castillo in *Miami Vice*, for example, and Jimmy Smits as slick, articulate lawyer Victor Sifuentes in *L.A. Law*. During the past three years, Latinos have been deeply involved in the production of a number of generally well-received films, such as *La Bamba*, *Born in East L.A.*, *Stand and Deliver*, and *The Milagro Beanfield War*.

Could we be entering a new era in which Chicanos and other U.S. Hispanics take at least partial control of their own media image destinies and, in the process, influence the media image of Mexico and the rest of Latin America? The signs suggest hope, but history cautions against too much optimism. Such hopes were previously raised during the first outburst of Chicano filmmaking, with such movies as *Zoot Suit* (1981), *Seguín* (1982), and the gripping *The Ballad of Gregorio Cortez* (1982). None of these movies dealt significantly with Mexico, however. But now Richard "Cheech" Marín has turned his special comic talents to the more serious subject of Mexican undocumented immigration in *Born in East L.A.*, while Luis Valdez has moved from the Chicano gangs of *Zoot Suit* to the pursuit of the American Dream as embodied in the short life of signer Ritchie Valens (nee Ricardo Valenzuela) in *La Bamba*. Both films also touch Mexico, but neither glorifies it.

In *Born in East L.A.*, Tijuana remains the dangerous and in some respects corrupt Mexican border of Hollywood lore, but it is also filled with good folks. American-born Chicano Rudy Robles, who has mistakenly been deported by *la migra*, discovers personal identity in Mexican culture and respect for the Mexican people. Yet

---

[56]A generally positive evaluation of *AKA Pablo* by a thoughtful Chicano scholar is Reynaldo F. Macías, "AKA Pablo: Stereotypes Revisited or Archie Bunker in Mexican Drag?" (report for the NBC Television Research Division, August 1984, mimeographed).

ultimately Mexico is a place to be left behind. In the film's climax, Rudy marches back into the United States amid an army of undocumented immigrants who pour into the promised land, backed by Neil Diamond singing "America." For Ritchie Valens in *La Bamba*, Tijuana provides a source of musical inspiration for his biggest hit. But it is also a source of temptation and danger. In short, it has yet to be proven that the apparent rise of Chicano filmmakers will mean a significant improvement in the film image of Mexico.

There are further signs of caution as well. During the summer of 1987 a movie trade magazine carried a casting notice for the film *Strange Justice*, requesting Hispanic actors to audition for two roles, one a "Hispanic wifebeater," the other "Latin, dark hair, handsome ... womanizer."[57] As yet, optimism is not entirely warranted.

This brings us back to the original question. What has been Hollywood's contribution to the public image of Mexico and *mexicanos*? One conclusion stands out with crystal clarity. Hollywood's Mexico and Hollywood's Mexicans have seldom been the primary focus of films. Although Hollywood has made thousands of movies that include Mexicans or Mexico (as well as Latinos and other areas of Latin America), it has made relatively few films that are truly about these subjects. Mexico and Mexicans—and to a lesser extent other Latinos—have served principally as colorful and challenging background scenery, as convenient devices, as iconographic conventions, and as surrogates for the United States.

For Hollywood, Mexico has been an ideal movie arena—a geographically contiguous, perceptually mysterious, and often turbulent nation with a physically identifiable, linguistically challenging, and culturally different people. And Mexicans have been the perfect vehicles for the filmic structuring of Anglo-American challenges, responses, dilemmas, resolutions, and ideological expositions. While plots have taken myriad forms, the almost inevitable underlying message has been the explicit or implicit reassertion of Anglo-American mental, physical, and moral superiority. To date, in short, Hollywood at best has been only an occasional force for creating a better understanding of Mexico and at worst has contributed to a distorted American popular view of our neighbor to the south.

---

[57]Antonio Mejías-Rentas, "Latinos Making Film History," *Latin Journal*, 10-16 September 1987, p. 2.

5

Mexico in U.S. Primary and Secondary Schools

Gerald Greenfield

INTRODUCTION

A discussion of cultural images of Mexico in U.S. pre-collegiate education must proceed from an appreciation of several larger contextual and structural factors. Broadly conceived, this issue merges with one that has received considerable discussion over the past few years, the international awareness or "literacy" of American school children. From commissioned studies to government critiques, articles assail an abysmally low level of international education in U. S. public schools. As the summary introduction to an investigation of public school students' awareness of and attitudes toward other nations observed: "On the knowledge findings alone, the pervasive ignorance about the Middle East and Africa, the lack of knowledge about Western Europe, are serious matters by any standard."[1] The admittedly inadequate level of instruction for foreign areas as a whole should serve, then, as a reference point in evaluating the portrayal of any specific country.

A second reference point resides in distinctions between knowledge and attitudes. Education specialists recognize the importance of the affective domain, the area in which prejudice and stereotype

---

[1] Robert Leestma, introduction to *Other Nations, Other People: A Survey of Student Interests, Knowledge, Attitudes, and Perceptions*, by Lewis Pike and T.S. Barrows (Princeton: Educational Testing Service, 1979), p. xii.

dwell. Much of our approach to higher education is predicated on the belief—indeed the faith—that communicating accurate, unbiased information while stressing the development of analytical skills will produce reasoning individuals capable of informed judgments. Such expectations often fly in the face of experience. Much of the information and methodologies presented in schools remains tightly compartmentalized in students' minds, isolated from the more general inchoate world of attitudes. For example, no matter how many times college-level historians may stress the multiple forces and factors relevant to an understanding of immigration to the United States, successive generations of students insist on the nearly exclusive primacy of a search for religious or political freedom.

This suggests that we must concern ourselves not only with the facts presented, but with the manner of their presentation if we are to more closely approximate the cultural images thereby promoted. Frances FitzGerald observed with regard to the impact of textbook learning: "what sticks to the memory from those textbooks is not any particular series of facts, but an atmosphere, an impression, a tone."[2] And as another global education specialist has noted:

> We organize information into our viewpoints based on our values and attitudes, and these ... are primarily the result of an individual's past experience. In fact, when a person has formed an image of another culture, and others in his group share these views, there is a strong tendency for that person to simply disregard any information that is inconsistent with those views.[3]

The issue of attitude formation in turn suggests that those concerned with questions of cultural image must identify their various sources. Within the public schools we may look at teachers, texts, and readers as primary ingredients, but there also exists an interactional world within the classroom that reflects the specific mix of ethnic factors among the student body. For example, at an individual level, a strongly positive association with a

---

[2]*America Revised* (Boston, 1979), p. 16, quoted by Dan B. Fleming in "Latin America and the United States, What Do United States History Textbooks Tell Us?" *Social Studies*, July/August 1982:168.
[3]George Otero, *Teaching about Perception: The Arabs*, Cultural Studies Series, vol. 1 (Denver, Colo.: Center for Teaching International Relations, Denver University, 1977), p. iii.

Mexican-American student might well prove more influential in attitude formation than any textbook treatment. Furthermore, at any grade level the classroom never forms the totality of the learning environment, especially with regard to attitudes. Here the media, particularly television, play an especially important role along with direct experience with peoples of other countries.

Finally, we must appreciate the various limitations inherent in the structure of public education and the place of social studies and foreign language curricula, the two areas which typically comprise the formal knowledge base for students in matters pertaining to images of other countries. The sorry state of foreign language instruction in the United States has long evoked concern among those interested in international studies. More recently new voices of concern have been raised as the maintenance of U.S. power and primacy seems imperiled by assertive new actors in Europe, Asia, and even Latin America. But the translation of concern into action, if indeed that is to occur, will require some time. For the nonce, foreign language instruction remains limited at all levels of public education, including the collegiate. As for the social studies, it should readily be apparent that presenting history, geography, political science, anthropology, sociology, and psychology under a common rubric presents problems in terms of teacher preparedness as well as of subject matter coverage.

The pattern changes at the secondary school level where the social studies emerge as independent disciplines and students may choose among several different courses in a particular field of study. This proves typical of history, where one finds such offerings as U.S., world, and even Russian history. But even at the secondary level, given competing demands of other subject areas, the comprehensiveness of the social studies program in such areas as history, geography, and political science remains limited.

PRECOLLEGIATE INSTRUCTION ON LATIN AMERICA

If precollegiate public education in the United States is generally weak with regard to social studies and foreign languages, and also reveals itself to be particularly weak in the field of international studies, the Latin American area suffers the exaggerated impact of these characteristics. Previous studies indicate serious inadequacies in the portrayal of Latin America in public school texts and in readers intended for a public school audience. Dan B. Fleming, investigating textbook treatment of United States-Latin

American relations with regard to such key issues as the Mexican War, the Panama Canal, the Good Neighbor Policy, and military interventions, concludes that:

> The perspective of the Latin American countries is given little attention in most books and the cultures of the region are ignored ... they fail to reveal the hostility and distrust built up in Latin America towards the United States as a result of our policies there over the past century or more.[4]

A similar study by Nancy Anderson and Rochelle Beck considered thirty children's books and texts in terms of their coverage of Central America.[5] The authors summarize the findings of a panel of expert reviewers who were asked to evaluate these materials concluding that:

> the children's books and learning materials included in this study leave students poorly prepared to understand events in Central America, confused about the countries and governments there, and alienated from Central American people and their cultures. The overwhelming majority of currently used texts and children's books perpetuate ignorance and distortions about Central America.[6]

Similarly my own recent survey of textbook treatment of Latin America found multiple problems of coverage, particularly in terms of a tone and outlook which often assumed the moral superiority of U.S. values and actions and focused heavily on the exotic or the negative.[7]

MEXICO IN U.S. PUBLIC SCHOOLS

What then of Mexico? Does its proximate location and the imprint of its culture on, and long-standing relationship with the United States make it a special case that escapes the limitations identified in the preceding discussion? Unfortunately, the failure

---

[4]Fleming, "Latin America," p. 171.

[5]"Central America by the Book, What Children are Learning," *Social Education*, February 1983, pp. 102-109.

[6]Ibid, p. 109.

[7]Gerald Michael Greenfield, "Latin America," *Social Education*, September 1986, pp. 351-356.

of this hypothesis is immediate and resounding. Mexico and things Mexican fare no better than other world areas, and in some cases it would appear that proximity and a sense of familiarity have led to the generation and dissemination of stereotypical images.

In 1979 Pike and Barrows administered a survey designed to assess both knowledge and attitudes about other world nations among fourth-, eighth-, and twelfth-grade students in the United States.[8] The universe comprised twelve countries: the United States, England, France, Spain, Japan, Mexico, India, Israel, China, the Soviet Union, Egypt, and East Germany. When asked what country they would most want to visit, 59 percent of fourth graders chose Mexico, the highest percentage recorded for any nation.[9] This preference became even stronger as a response to the question, "what country would you most like to study?" Here, 68 percent selected Mexico, followed by Japan, with 53 percent.[10] By the eighth grade, Mexico had yielded its primacy but still was near the top of the list of countries students would like to visit or study. For high-school seniors, however, Mexico hovered near or at the bottom as a response to these questions.[11]

A more significant aspect of student attitudes toward Mexico emerged from questions designed to measure conceptions of nations and their people. Global categories for the fourth grade included desirable, rich/strong, and perceived similarity to the United States. Among the twelve nations, Mexico stood third in desirability, right behind the United States and England. Students tended to see its people as fairly similar to themselves. They ranked Mexico sixth place with regard to wealth.[12] Categories in the eighth and twelfth grades included: desirable people, rich/strong, desirable nation, small nation, unfree. For students at this level, Mexico proved less attractive, ranking fifth as a desirable nation and sixth in terms of its people. They saw it as one of the poorest and weakest of the nations. Mexico largely maintained its low rankings in the twelfth-grade survey.[13]

---

[8]Lewis W. Pike and Thomas S. Barrows, *Other Nations, Other Peoples: A Survey of Student Interests, Knowledge, Attitudes and Perceptions* (Washington, D.C.: U.S. Dept. of Health, Education, and Welfare). The study surveyed a representative national sample of U.S. public schools.
[9]Ibid., p. vii. The percentages were: Mexico, 59; Canada, 52; England, France, Spain, Japan, 49; India, 41.
[10]Ibid.
[11]Ibid. The percentages for country to visit were: England, 46; Canada, 38; France, 37; Italy, 30; Spain, 27; Mexico, 24; Japan, 22.
[12]Ibid., table 44.
[13]Ibid., tables 45 and 46.

A follow-up study by Haas and Clary published in 1985 repli-
cated these findings for the state of Arkansas.[14] In this study Canada
received the highest number of significant responses in terms of
information level among fourth graders, but Mexico rested
comfortably at a middle level on a par with Egypt, China, and
England. In terms of images, students at this grade level tended
to view all nations except the Soviet Union in positive terms. The
author speculated that this occurred, "perhaps because the students
perceived of the U.S.A. in emotionally positive terms and trans-
ferred that image to nations that were considered friends of the
U.S.A."[15] This orientation retained some constancy through
succeeding grade levels. At the eighth grade level, given this
generally favorable overall outlook, however,the descriptors most
commonly chosen for Mexico were "poor," "peaceful," and "weak."
Moreover, Mexico ranked near the bottom in terms of student
knowledge, along with such nations as Israel, East Germany, and
Egypt.[16] Apparently, eight years of education had served to reduce
relative student interest in and awareness of Mexico!

Is this precipitous drop in interest a reflection of boredom
produced by overexposure? Hardly. Here again Pike and Barrows
provides some guidance. Presented with a list of fifteen nations
(Mexico, Canada, France, Spain, Italy, West Germany, East Germany,
the Soviet Union, Taiwan, Japan, India, Israel, and Egypt) and asked
to note those they recently had studied, eighth graders most often
chose the Soviet Union, followed by England. For this group,
Mexico ranked eighth. By the twelfth grade Mexico had fallen one
place.[17] This same survey found that in grades eight and twelve,
U.S. and world history were overwhelmingly the most common
history courses. In neither of these history courses did Mexico
receive major attention.[18] How often, then, and in what context do
units on Mexico appear in the course of twelve years of precollegiate education?

My own recent telephone survey of state department of education social studies supervisors provides some additional

---

[14]Mary E. Haas and Eldon Clary, "The Perception of Other Nations by Students in
Northwestern Arkansas," Research Report, Arkansas Tech University, 15 March 1985.
Nations included in the study were the United States, England, France, Russia, India,
China, Spain, Japan, Israel, East Germany, Mexico, and Egypt.
[15]Ibid., p. 9.
[16]Ibid., pp. 10, 12, 19.
[17]Pike and Barrows, p. 12.
[18]Ibid., p. xii and table 53.

insights.[19] Results from thirty-eight states suggest the absence of any special emphasis on Mexico, although this assessment remains somewhat uncertain due to the lack of uniformity within states. Most states are nonmandated, meaning that local school districts remain free to structure specific curricula within general guidelines developed by the state department of education. Several states presently are developing guidelines that call for increased attention to global education. None of the states responding to this survey, however, indicated that Mexico would be the special focus of such a program. Moreover, social studies supervisors emphasized that guidelines remained essentially exercises in goal setting and did not necessarily imply implementation. For a comprehensive and accurate appraisal of the current level of instruction related to Mexico, one would have to survey individual school districts. Perhaps the most disturbing aspect of the telephone survey is thus the degree to which state-level officials remained uninformed as to activities of the individual school districts.

In general, however, Latin American units typically appear somewhere during grades four through seven, most commonly in the sixth and seventh grades. Here, the general vehicle is a focus on the Western Hemisphere, which includes Canada as well as Latin America. At the middle or high school level, Latin America sometimes receives separate attention in the ninth grade. Otherwise, it appears in some specialized elective courses. Above the primary grade level, then, the major point of contact with the region as a whole occurs in the context of courses on U.S. or world history. In almost all cases, those responding to the survey said that Mexico would receive more discussion than any other nation in Latin America. State social studies supervisors, however, generally did not think that special materials were used for such courses. They indicated that major text series all included volumes dealing with the Western Hemisphere or with Latin America.

Indiana reported a special unit for kindergarten through the third grade, "Understanding Our Neighbors to the South," developed through Indiana University's Center for Latin American and Caribbean Studies, and an intermediate-to-senior high school unit,

---

[19]The survey asked whether the state had instruction of Latin America and, if so, at what grade level. It repeated this question for Mexico. It also solicited information regarding teaching materials. States for which no information was compiled included Alaska, Arkansas, Delaware, Florida, Hawaii, Louisiana, Massachusetts, Missouri, North Carolina, Rhode Island, West Virginia, and Wyoming.

"Understanding Our Partners in Trade, the Early Mexicans," sponsored by the Indiana Department of Commerce's International Trade Division. Connecticut reported that West Hartford school district had an International Center, and that children in grades five and six go to Mexico for a week.

Finally, almost all supervisors supported the importance of devoting greater attention to global studies in general, and many suggested that our close neighbors—Mexico and Canada—certainly ought to receive particular attention in such programs.

IMAGES FROM TEXTS AND READERS

Given the infrequent incidence of specially designed materials at the state level, it is safe to conclude that major national textbooks and readers comprise the major source of information and images regarding Mexico. An analysis of a representative sample of these materials reveals a mixture of strengths and weaknesses, as well as some consistent problems. Looking at the high school level, as noted earlier, world and U.S. history are the dominant courses. The title "world history" is usually a misnomer in that western civilization serves as the major focus. In such courses, Latin America recedes from the forefront after the age of exploration and discovery. Students may conclude, therefore, that Mexico has little importance in, or impact on, the course of world events except for the glories of the Maya and Aztecs. The way in which Mexico typically appears in U.S. history also creates some image problems. Again the early Indian civilizations and Spanish patterns of colonization constitute the initial points of exposure. After that, as the logic of a U.S. focus demands, Mexico appears only as it relates to issues or processes important to the United States. Hence, the Texas question and Mexican War receive attention in chapters on westward expansion or manifest destiny. Other typical points of inclusion come in relation to the Monroe Doctrine—particularly the French intervention, the Latin American policy of Woodrow Wilson, World War I, and the Zimmermann telegram. Oil expropriation and contemporary issues of undocumented workers also are common subjects. At best, the Mexican experience thus emerges as a reflex to larger U.S. concerns, and at worst as the story of a weak and corrupt nation that in one era attempted to impede American expansionism, took away American property in another, and that now exports its problems to the United States.

Representative of the presentation of the Texas question and ensuing war is the account by noted historian Henry F. Graff: "The Texans tried to get along with the Mexican Government." However, because Santa Anna established a military dictatorship, the Texans revolted. After the Alamo—where the students are reminded, such great men as Davey Crockett and Sam Bowie died— "Sam Houston led an army of angry Texans against Santa Anna." Then, after Santa Anna agreed to independence for Texas in order to save his own life, the Americans in Texas pushed for annexation to the United States. With the southern border of Texas in dispute, President Polk sent troops to the Rio Grande. "Mexican troops, making the first move, crossed the Rio Grande." War broke out, the United States won, and the Rio Grande was set as the southern border of the United States.[20] This rendition, which also stresses the United States' payment of $15 million to Mexico, clearly defines the issues as Texas and freedom, thereby confirming a popular-culture view both common and congenial to the United States. Approaches of this type, which present simplistic causal relationships and clearly identify heroes and villains, typify most accounts of this issue at all grade levels.

Portrayals of Wilson's Latin American policy also evince a sympathetic approach with regard to Mexico. As a recent Macmillan high school text explains, Woodrow Wilson attempted to help the Mexicans: "Wilson decided that he favored the interests of the 85 percent of the Mexican people struggling toward liberty over the interests of foreign investors." So, despite the fact that Americans "who had invested almost $1 billion in Mexico favored Huerta because they believed he would keep order,"[21] Wilson stood against that unsavory dictator.

This text goes on to note the clash at Veracruz resulting from the United States' attempt to enforce its embargo, which ends with mediation of the ABC powers, and the confirmation of the U.S. demand "that Huerta must go." This account concludes that:

> Although Wilson's Mexican policy was well intentioned, it won the United States no friends. Latin Americans looked upon what they regarded as

---

[20]Henry F. Graff, *This Great Nation* (Chicago: Riverside Publishing Company, 1983), pp. 326-27.

[21]*Heritage of Freedom*, vol. 2, History of the United States from 1877 (New York: Scribner Educational Publishers, Macmillan, 1986), p. 201.

Wilson's 'moral imperialism' with no more favor
than Roosevelt's Big Stick diplomacy.[22]

What are students likely to conclude from this account? The United
States had acted in favor of altruistic, abstract principle and against
the economic interests of its own citizens. It also had accepted
arbitration. What rational grounds existed, therefore, for Latin
American distress?

Interestingly, the high school texts present a less emotion-laden
account of the contemporary question of undocumented workers.
The Great Nation, for example, stresses the cooperative efforts of
both the U.S. and Mexican governments to deal with this issue, as
well as the hope that economic growth in Mexico will "create new
jobs for Mexican workers."[23] A possible explanation is that the
presence of large numbers of Mexican and Mexican-American
children in the United States and the large amount of contemporary discussion of the immigration issue has sensitized authors and
publishers. Events of a distant past, however, already have entered
into a popular historical understanding. There they remain frozen,
untouched by contemporary sensitivities to issues of multicultural
education.

At the primary and middle school levels, textbooks focusing
on Latin America often suffer from a lack of balance and an
emphasis on the exotic. Typically, they emphasize only a few prominent features or themes, often those viewed as most apt to arouse
student interest. In part this results from major problems of coverage alluded to earlier. For instance, Heath's sixth and seventh grade
series, *The World Today,*[24] has a Latin American unit that takes only
seven pages to discuss Mexico from pre-Columbian civilization to
the present day. Obviously, such highly telescoped accounts, typical
of many primary school texts, do not provide much opportunity
for comprehensive, leisurely discussion. They present, therefore,
a very difficult problem of selection. No matter how informed the
author, however, any such selection must do considerable injus-
tice to the goal of a holistic portrayal of any nation.

---

[22]Ibid.
[23]Graff, *This Great Nation,* p. 707.
[24]Barbara Reque et al., *The World Today,* Heath Social Studies Series (Lexington, Mass:
D.C. Heath, 1985).

Looking at *The World Today*, it is difficult to take exception to the topics that are presented: the Aztecs, conquest, problems of nation-building in the nineteenth century, and the impact of the Revolution. It also includes portrayals of Hidalgo, Benito Juárez, and Porfirio Díaz, and the tone of the discussion does seem balanced. It presents as a central idea that "Mexico and the countries of Central America became independent nations, but at first there was little change in the region." It concludes that "the ejidos, the school system and the other reforms that began in 1920 have made life better for many in Mexico," but that "it will be many years before the problems that began far back in Mexico's history are finally solved."[25]

But if it is possible to achieve a degree of balance within the limitations inherent in a primary level social studies unit, it is far easier to slip into simplification. For example, dealing with issues of poverty and development, one elementary text observed that: "Mexico has been called a 'poor man seated on a bag of gold,'"[26] while another, dealing with the Texas question, opined that "many Americans felt the Mexican-controlled lands should belong to the United States" but never discussed why or by what right they ought to have felt that way. The impression of U.S. reasonableness is further promoted when the text, continuing to discuss continental expansion, notes that the United States offered $30 million for California and New Mexico, "but Mexico would not sell these lands."[27]

Even materials designed to promote cultural understanding among primary school students can create or promote stereotypical images. *Mexican*, "a book of culturally based activities for K-6 children,"[28] presents a social studies activity on Mexican clothing in which children make paper dolls and clothes. This book advises teachers that "clothing worn by people of Mexico in the large cities and towns is quite similar to the clothing worn in the United States."[29] It then describes village and holiday clothing.

---

[25]Ibid., p. 122. This section also presents a quote from Zapata, "it is better to die on your feet than to live on your knees," and suggests that students be asked to explain the meaning.

[26]*Our World and Its Peoples* (Boston: Allyn and Bacon, 1981), p. 191.

[27]*The Making of Our America* (Boston: Allyn and Bacon, 1982), p. 300.

[28]Barbara Schubert and Marlene Bird, *Mexican* (San Jose, Calif.: Reflections and Images, 1976).

[29]Ibid., p. 36.

But when it comes to the prescribed activity for children, only the traditional garb receives emphasis. Men are clothed either in the "national costume," of a dark blue *charro* suit, or in cotton shirts and slacks with huaraches, sombreros, and serapes. Women, children are told, "wear blouses and long, full skirts. They cover their heads with fringed shawls called rebozos."[30]

Perhaps the most inadequate coverage of Mexico—that promoting the most negative images—appears in supplementary readers, especially those designed for elementary school children. In *A Hispanic Heritage: A Guide to Juvenile Books about Hispanic People and Cultures*, Isabel Schon reviews forty-eight books about Mexico.[31] She rates only one-third of these as noteworthy. Several others emerge as reasonably good, albeit not outstanding. However, an equally large number receive scathing evaluations for their inaccurate, outdated, or unbalanced discussions.[32] My own survey of the twenty readers for grades three through seven available in the local public library projects an even bleaker picture. Poor village children appear with depressing frequency, and almost all illustrations stress "traditional" portrayals: burros, serapes, sandals, and sombreros. (See chart on following pages.)

The portrayal of Mexico in U.S. public education, whether judged by content, coverage, or tone, clearly has some serious flaws. Given the growing importance of Mexico as an actor in Latin America and the world, and the pronounced interdependence of the United States and Mexico, the problems revealed by this review are particularly disturbing.

---

[30]Isabel Schon (Metuchen, N.J.: Scarecrow, 1980).
[31]Her review of *Manuela's Birthday* (by Laura Bannon, 1972, intended for grades K-3) is representative: "This story combines all the curios of Mexico in thirty pages with ridiculous illustrations: sombreros, barefooted Indians, burros."
[32]Ibid., p. 48.

Public Library Illustrated Stories
Grade Levels 3-7

Author	Title/Date	Storyline	Illustrations
Brenner, Anita	A Hero by Mistake (n.d.)	Story of a very frightened Indian	Thirty simple line drawings. Indian symbols, barefeet and sandals, burro, bugle, and townspeople.
Carr, Elizabeth	The Mystery of the Aztec Idol (1959)	Mexican adventure and mystery for an American visitor	No illustrations.
Clymer, Eleanor	Santiago's Silver Mine (1973)	Poor boy helps archeologists	Nineteen black and white sketches. Bare feet and sandals, straw hats, inside of church, marketplace with tourists, burro and cactus.
Coatsworth, Elizabeth	The Noble Doll (1961)	A little girl and her doll celebrate Christmas	Sixteen color drawings. Courtyard and marketplace, Christmas parade with candles, barefeet and sandals, burros, and the breaking of a piñata.
Coleman, Hila	That's The Way It Is, Amigo (1975)	Runaway American finds a friend in Mexico	Fifteen black and white illustrations. Varied aspects of Mexico from temple ruins to poor rancho.
Credle, Ellis	Little Pest Pico (1969)	Mexican boy purchases a parrot that sings the Mexican National Anthem when the President of Mexico comes to visit	Twenty-five color and sepia illustrations. Small village, barefeet and sandals, sombreros, burros, marketplace, ancient loaded bus, and town-square celebration.
Fante, John and Rudolph Borchert	Bravo, Burro! (1970)	Young boy finds burro and together they become involved in adventure	Eleven charcoal drawings. Boy in sandals and straw hat. Burros pulling overloaded carts, wildlife, schoolyard, bull ring, and matador.

Public Library Illustrated Stories (continued)
Grade Levels 3-7

Author	Title/Date	Storyline	Illustrations
Flora, James	*The Fabulous Firework Family* (1955)	Mexican family prepares fireworks display for a town celebration	Twenty-six very busy illustrations. People wearing simple sandals, sombreros, and serapes. Many fiesta scenes.
Kalnay, Francis	*It Happened in Chichipica* (1971)	Young Mexican boy growing up in small town	Eleven black and white illustrations. Boy with serape, and straw hat. Burro, birds, fishing, and overloaded bus.
Kjelgaard, Jim	*Tigre* (1961)	Young Mexican boy protects his goats from a tiger	Eighteen black and white illustrations. Barefeet and straw hat, wildlife, birds, crocodile, tiger, hunting with spear and guns.
Laughlin, Florence	*The Horse from Topolo* (1966)	Two young Americans visit Mexico with their archeologist-aunt	Seventeen black and white illustrations. Temple ruins, statuary, and one market scene with people laughing, flowers etc.
Means, Florence	*Emmy and the Blue Door* (1959)	College student joins missionary group to help poor Mexican farm workers	Thirteen pen and ink illustrations. Several action pictures, Mexicans wear sombreros, serapes, barefeet and sandals.
Nixon, Joan	*The Mystery of the Grinning Idol* (1965)	Mystery for a young American girl visiting Mexico for the first time	Thirteen pen and ink illustrations. Action scenes, marketplace, overloaded burro, overloaded bus, and fiesta scene.
O'Dell, Scott	*The Treasure of Topo-El-Bampo* (1972)	Historical fiction about a poor town near a silver mine	Thirty-one realistic drawings. Poor people in barefeet and serapes. Fiesta scene with fireworks, mining process, horses, and lots of overworked burros.

Public Library Illustrated Stories (continued)
Grade Levels 3-7

Author	Title/Date	Storyline	Illustrations
Polito, Leo	*Juanita* (1948)	Little Mexican girls enjoy a fiesta and parade	Fifteen simple color illustrations. Mexican dress and handcrafts, parade, blessing from the priest, happy smiling faces, and lots of flowers.
Rowlands, Florence	*School for Julio* (1968)	Poor farm boy writes a letter to the President of Mexico, requesting that a school be built in his small neighborhood town	Twenty-one simple color illustrations. Barefoot, straw-hatted farmers picking harvest, caring for animals, building school, and raising the flag.
Steinbeck, John	*The Pearl* (1966)	Steinbeck's classic	Five black and white illustrations. Poor man and woman in surroundings.
Stolz Mary	*Juan* (1970)	Poor orphan boy receives his wish from American couple, a pair of red rubber boots for the rainy season	Eight black and white illustrations. Poor children from orphanage, barefeet and sandals, market scene, and piñata breaking.
Stone, Helen V.	*Pablo the Potter* (1969)	Poor young boy learns about growing up by helping a friend	Fifteen charcoal sketches. Many market scenes, serapes, barefeet and sandals, pottery making, overloaded burro.
Vavra, Robert	*Pizorro* (n.d.)	Poor farm boy wishes for a burro to help him wish chores	Sixty-one color photographs. Sandaled boy, serapes, straw hats, marketplace, cactus, burro, and many beautiful landscapes.

About the Contributors

John Bailey is Professor and Chairman of the Department of Government at Georgetown University and has published various items on themes of interest groups, administrative politics, and policy-making in Latin America. His recent publications include "Can the PRI Be Reformed? Decentralizing Candidate Selection," in Judith Gentleman, ed., *Mexican Politics in Transition* (Westview, 1987) and a book, *Governing Mexico: The Statecraft of Crisis Management*, which was co-published by Macmillan (London) and St. Martin's (New York) in 1988.

Professor Bailey has served since 1980 as Chairman of the Advanced Area Studies Seminar on Mexico at the Foreign Service Institute and has contributed papers to the Department of State, the most recent being "Reform of the Mexican Political System: Prospects for Change in 1987-88," (July, 1987) and "Mexican Politics after the 1988 Elections," (September 1988).

John Coatsworth is a senior member of the history faculty and Director of the Center for Latin American Studies at the University of Chicago. He is one of the world's leading specialists on Mexican economic history, and has published three major books and dozens of articles in this field. He is currently Chair of the Joint Committee on Latin American Studies of the Social Science Research Council and the American Council of Learned Societies.

Christine Contee is a Fellow of the Overseas Development Council, as well as the Director of Public Affairs. She is the author of several articles on the U.S. foreign assistance program and public opinion, including *What Americans Think: Views on Development and U.S. Third World Relations* (ODC/InterAction, 1987).

Carlos Cortés is a Professor of History at the University of California, Riverside. The recipient of two book awards and numerous fellowships, he also received his university's Distinguished Teaching Award and the California Council for the Humanities' 1980 Distinguished California Humanist Award. Among his many publications are *Gaúcho Politics in Brazil, A Filmic Approach to the Study of Historical Dilemmas,* and *Three Perspectives on Ethnicity,* while he has edited three book series on Latinos in the United States. Cortés is currently working on a three-volume study of the history of the U.S. motion picture treatment of ethnic groups, foreign nations, and world cultures. He has lectured widely throughout the United States, Latin America, and Europe, while also serving as a government, educational, media, and business consultant.

Rosario Green is director of the Commission on Foreign Affairs of the National Executive Council of the Partido Revolucionario Institucional (PRI). She studied economics and international relations at the National Autonomous University of Mexico, at El Colegio de México, at Columbia University in New York and at the Instituto para la Integración Latinoamericana (INTAL) in Buenos Aires. She has been a professor at El Colegio de México and, from 1982 to 1988, director of the Matías Romero Institute of Diplomatic Studies. Ms. Green has published ten books, including a prescient analysis of Mexico's foreign indebtedness—*El endeudamiento público externo de México: 1950-1973; Estado y banca transnacional en México*; and, most recently, *La deuda externa de México de 1973 a 1988: de la abundancia a la escasez de créditos.* She has written articles for academic reviews and journalistic media in various languages. Ms. Green has also been a consultant to the United Nations and to the Sistema Económico Latinoamericano.

Gerald Greenfield is professor of history and international studies at the University of Wisconsin, Parkside where he is the Director of the Center for International Studies. He earned a Ph.D. in Latin American History from Indiana University, Bloomington in 1975.

A specialist in urban history, he co-edited *Latin American Labor Organizations*, and currently is editing *A Handbook of Latin American Urbanization*. He has published articles in scholarly journals and books in Brazil, Argentina, and the United States.

Prior to attending graduate school, he taught junior high school in Brooklyn, New York for three years. He has retained his interest in pre-collegiate education, particularly as related to Latin America, and has conducted workshops for public school teachers and spoken at state social studies conventions. He currently is revising and updating a sixth-grade social studies text, *The Western Hemisphere, Yesterday and Today*, for Silver, Burdett and Ginn.

Carlos Rico is presently a professor and researcher at El Colegio de México's International Studies Center and an advisor to the North American Studies Program of the Instituto Latinoamericano de Estudios Transnacionales. He attended El Colegio de México from 1969 to 1972, receiving his degree in International Relations. He completed his doctorate in 1980 in the Department of Government at Harvard University. He has been a professor at the Universidad Iberoamericana, the Universidad Nacional Autónoma de México, the Centro de Investigación y Docencia Económicas, the Facultad Latinoamericana de Ciencias Sociales, Duke University, and the University of North Carolina-Chapel Hill. He was an advisor to Mexico's Foreign Relations Minister from February 1972 to December 1975, and he has been a member of the Mexican delegation in diverse international forums. He has published many books and articles on U.S.-Mexican and inter-American relations.

Peter H. Smith is professor of political science and Simón Bolívar professor of Latin American studies at the University of California, San Diego. Born in Brooklyn, New York, he graduated from Harvard College in 1961 and earned a Ph.D. from Columbia University in 1966. A specialist on long-run processes of political change, Mr. Smith has written books on Argentina and on empirical methodology. His best-known work on Mexico is *Labyrinths of Power*, a study of elite recruitment and mobility. He has also co-authored a textbook entitled *Modern Latin America*. Mr. Smith has served as a department chair and academic associate dean at the University of Wisconsin and at MIT, and he is past president of the Latin American Studies Association. He was professor of history and political science at the Massachusetts Institute of Technology before joining the faculty of UC-San Diego.